THE GILL HISTORY OF

General Editors: JAMES LYDON, PH D.
MARGARET MACCURTAIN, PH D.

Other titles in the series

ANGLO-NORMAN IRELAND

c1100–1318

Michael Dolley

GILL AND MACMILLAN

Published by
Gill and Macmillan Ltd
2 Belvedere Place
Dublin 1
and in association with the
Macmillan
Group of Publishing Companies

© Michael Dolley, 1972

Cover design by Cor Klaasen

7171 0560 X

Printed and bound in the Republic of Ireland by the
Book Printing Division of Smurfit Print and Packaging Limited
Dublin

Do shliocht Bhearnaird naomh
sa Mhainistir Mhóir
a d'fhan dílis do Mhuire
trí luainní an tsaoil.

Contents

Foreword

THE study of Irish history has changed greatly in recent decades, as more evidence becomes available and new insights are provided by the growing number of historians. It is natural, too, that with each generation new questions should be asked about our past. The time has come for a new large-scale history. It is the aim of the Gill History of Ireland to provide this. This series of studies of Irish history, each written by a specialist, is arranged chronologically. But each volume is intended to stand on its own and no attempt has been made to present a uniform history. Diversity of analysis and interpretation is the aim; a group of young historians have tried to express the view of their generation on our past. It is the hope of the editors that the series will help the reader to appreciate in a new way the rich heritage of Ireland's history.

JAMES LYDON, PH D.
MARGARET MACCURTAIN, PH D.

Preface

THE book is an attempt to tell in simple outline the story of the political evolution of twelfth- and thirteenth-century Ireland. Very largely neglected are the constitutional, institutional and socio-economic aspects of the narrative, and this is deliberate inasmuch as in the fourth volume of the series they are treated by Mr Kenneth Nicholls with an authority to which I could never pretend. There is parallel neglect of most if not all of the ecclesiastical history of these critical centuries, and again the explanation is that Dr Jack Watt's fifth volume in the series will be concerning itself specifically with this integral strand in the history of mediaeval Ireland.

To depart from a highroad plotted half a century and more ago by Goddard Orpen has proved unexpectedly difficult—and by some it will doubtless be considered presumptuous—but I remain convinced that there is something to be gained by the deliberate' eschewal of whole chapters given over to the affairs of a particular province. No less obvious should be the present volume's indebtedness to the standard outline histories of Edmund Curtis and of Professor Jocelyn Otway-Ruthven. The one has worn in the event quite remarkably well, and is perhaps on the point of coming again into its own, while the other seems likely to be for years to come the historian's definitive account of the government of the Anglo-Irish colony in the centuries preceding Poynings.

More personal are my obligations to my mediaevalist

colleagues in the Queen's University of Belfast, Mr Jack Gray and Dr Lewis Warren, and it would be unthinkable for me not to pay tribute here to their kindly encouragement. Without this I am sure that I would never have ventured to essay any broader approach to the problems of Irish history than that implied by my own narrow and restrictive specialism. To the general editor of *The Gill History of Ireland's* mediaeval fascicles, Professor James Lydon, I am indebted for some pertinent comments on the original drafts, and for good advice which I fear I may not always have taken. In the same way I am more than grateful to the Cistercian Community of New Mellifont for the peace and quiet—and even inspiration—which enabled me to complete the greater part of the text in the course of a summer as sad and as traumatic for any conscientious teacher of the young as any that Belfast has been able to offer.

At this point, indeed, a few words may not be altogether out of place with respect to the relevance to Irish history as a whole of the twelfth and thirteenth centuries in particular, and it may be perhaps no harm if a little should be revealed in the process of the author's own aspirations and even prejudices. As it happens, these paragraphs are being penned at the end of the month when the great majority of the enfranchised Irish people endorsed their elected leaders' decision to enter into some closer association with Europe, and it was in the twelfth century, of course, that Ireland was for the first time brought—and perhaps too abruptly—by her princes and bishops into the mainstream of European affairs. Again, it was in the thirteenth century that England's preoccupation with Continental ambitions destroyed what was probably the last chance she was ever to have of achieving a total integration of Ireland into an English polity.

What we do well always to remember, too, is that the very concept of 'the two nations' which is seen with increasing clarity after the 1240s in itself represents an essential and critical victory of Irishness over the sought for imposition of a monolithic feudalism amounting to an alien way of life. Seen in this light it must be of minor importance—except perhaps to antiquarians—that the immigrant gallowglass was in point of fact just as destructive of the traditional fabric and values of a fossilised Gaelic society as the Anglo-Norman knight whom he was brought in to combat. If, too, it was not until early in the fourteenth century that Anglo-Irish patriots styling themselves 'English by blood' began formally to be indicted for treason by imported English servants of their common lord and king, already in the twelfth and certainly the thirteenth centuries we can confidently detect the genesis and consolidation of a colonial faction with interests far from coincident with those of the English Crown.

In the same way, just as in earlier centuries the fears of the Leinstermen are a better key to our understanding of events in Ireland than all the pretensions of the kings of Tara and of Cashel, so the unfolding failure of John's plan for eventual integration is more profitably studied against the background of the mounting resentments of the increasingly embattled Englishry—not to mention the inevitably satellite Welsh. The apogee of English power in Ireland could well have been in 1245 when the dutiful Felim O Connor crossed to Deganwy as Henry III's man, but by 1249 not even the débâcle of Athenry can quite disguise the fact that the tide had turned, and that there was evolving a tacit abandonment of the Angevin dream of an Ireland with lords of Gaelic and of Anglo-Norman extraction indistinguishable the one from the other in their common subordination to the will of the English king.

Michael Dolley
The Queen's University
Béal Feirste, Festo S. Bedae, 1972

CONNACHT   The Historic Fifths

BREGA   Territories mentioned as such

ULSTER

ULIDIA

FERMANAGH

BREIFNE   FARNEY   ORIEL

MEATH

CONNACHT

BREGA

LEINSTER

OSSORY

THOMOND

DECIES

MUNSTER

DESMOND

The principal Irish territories mentioned in the text

1 Munster's Swansong

ON 15 July 1099, to shouts of 'God wills it', a random and ragged but reasonably representative array of the chivalry of Western Europe stormed Jerusalem. The First Crusade had ended, albeit ephemerally, Islamic occupation of the Holy Places. We should not be surprised that there were no Irishmen among these knights, and the event was in fact ignored by contemporary Irish chroniclers. Where Europe was concerned, Ireland was a land apart, and Irish society something quite unique. The Roman legions had refrained from undertaking a conquest of Ireland very largely because the Irish, unlike their British cousins, had not lifted their eyes to the affairs of their nearest neighbours, and five centuries later the bloodless conversion of the Irish to Christianity had had remarkably little influence on the shape, and indeed the ethos, of Irish society. Three centuries after Patrick the advent of the Vikings had seemed for a time likely to jerk Ireland into the mainstream of the development of northwestern Europe, but even in military defeat the Irish proved singularly successful in modifying the external forces that had seemed poised for their final dismemberment. By the tenth century the Norse in Ireland, the Ostmen as we may begin to call them, had surprisingly few direct contacts with Norway, while the eleventh-century triumph of the Danes in England meant that the predominantly Norwegian Ostmen were turned in on themselves even more. Clontarf (23 April 1014) was essentially a battle between Irishmen, the

Leinstermen who had provoked it having allied themselves with the equally embattled Ostmen of Dublin who in turn were able on this occasion to attract wide support from their cousins who had colonised Man and the Scottish Isles. This is not to say that the Vikings had not modified profoundly the whole structure and outlook if not the theory of Irish society. Two centuries of strife had seen the weaker elements going generally to the wall, and even a brutalisation of what seemed to survive intact. The real tragedy of Clontarf, though, was not the death of the aged Brian nicknamed Bóromha ('Brian Boru') but rather the fact that his Munstermen were so weakened by their Pyrrhic victory that other Irish dynasties were encouraged to compete for the prize of his new concept of a 'High Kingship' without being strong enough to secure let alone maintain it. Novel this institution might be, and even reprehensible where traditional liberties were concerned, but it might have evolved into a strong centralised monarchy capable of welding Ireland into an entity so formidable that Norman adventurers would have looked elsewhere for easy conquest.

By the year 1100 it should have been clear to all but the most partisan that not even a relatively strong and even enlightened O Brien king like Murtagh had the power to impose an effective personal sovereignty over Ireland as a whole. On the other hand, the old rivals in the race for the High Kingship, the O Melaghlin line of O Neill in Meath, were too weak even to pretend to the old Kingship of Tara which in its heyday had afforded a pretty satisfying overlordship of most though not all of the island. On the sidelines lurked almost sinisterly the new dynasty of Mac Murrough in South Leinster which in due course would throw up Dermot of the Foreigners, and the virtual obliteration of Leinster—and of the Leinster version of Irish history—in the first flush of the Anglo-Norman invasion of Ireland should not be allowed to blind us to the fact that an understanding of Leinster's fears is the best possible guide to the elucidation of the early twelfth-century history of Ireland as a whole. We should never forget that the two most important of the Norse cities in Ireland, Dublin and Waterford, had been founded and had flourished at the seaward extremities of the natural lines of fission between Leinster and Meath on the one hand, and Leinster and Munster on the other. The circumstance, too, that the Ostmen of Waterford had tended to throw in their lot with the O Briens meant that there was an increasing community of interest between the Mac Murroughs and the Dubliners, and especially when the centre of power in Leinster had shifted southwards. Both parties could feel embattled, as the Leinstermen had felt for centuries and with good reason, and even before the advent of the Norse the geographical position of Leinster had meant that of the Irish the Leinstermen had been the least resistant to influences from abroad. The virtual disappearance of Meath as a great power, moreover, meant that the hinterland of Dublin was of less critical importance for Leinster, whereas O Brien possession of Cashel posed a constant threat to her ill-defined western borders, and history as seen through the eyes of non-Leinster chroniclers has passed over far too lightly Dermot mac Mael na mBo's very real achievement when, within half a century of Clontarf, he salvaged a Leinster which would not only be viable but capable of becoming a very respectable third force in Irish politics of the twelfth century.

The essential challenge to Murtagh O Brien was made up of three quite disparate elements. First but perhaps not foremost were the dissidents within his own kin. A brother Dermot was quite spectacularly disloyal, but no less dangerous were certain cousins who felt and not without justification that they had been passed over for the king-ship. Secondly one must not forget that the O Briens enjoyed power in Munster at the expense of the Eoganachts who for centuries had held sway from Cashel over an area which in favourable circumstances might include large portions of Leinster and even Connacht. The tenth-century Eoganachts may have been a thoroughly degenerate house and one divided against itself, but they had learned much from adversity, and the very ramifications of their princely connections became now a source of strength rather than weakness. Discreetly but remorselessly there was being built up a new concentration of power in the area around Loch Lene where the precursors of the Mac Carthys of the thirteenth century represented a power in Desmond that the O Briens ignored at their peril. The third of the problems that confronted Murtagh O Brien was the circumstance that the heartland of Dalcassian power lay north of the Shannon in what is now east Clare, and so abutted directly on Connacht. Here the O Connors, after a period of near-eclipse at the hands of the O Flahertys based on Connemara and the O Rourkes established in Breifne, were on the point of exploding into the most powerful of all the province kings. Piquantly Murtagh himself had contributed much to the new O Connor menace by humbling the O Rourkes when the latter had sought to expand southeastwards into territory increasingly regarded by the O Briens as politically sensitive. In fact there was at this stage little real danger of O Brien interests in the Midlands being swamped by O Neill resurgence, the line of the O Melaghlins in Meath being in process of supersession by the more remote dynasty of the Mac Loughlins. Busily engaged in consolidating their power in mid-Ulster, the Mac Loughlins still were not strong enough to exercise sufficient power along the upper Shannon to have restrained the O Connors, let alone represented any real threat to O Brien ascendancy.

For an Irish king of this period Murtagh could be thought unusually outward looking. We are told in the *Annals of Inisfallen* how in 1105 he was sent 'a camel by the king of Alba', and, whatever our reservations as to the nature of the beast and the identification of the donor, the incident is one which suggests the international figure. In 1100 the hand of one of his daughters was sought successfully by Arnulf of Montgomery who was more than on the fringe of a conspiracy then being mounted against Henry I of England by the Norman lords of the Welsh Marches. His father Turlough had been written to in honorific terms by no less a Pope than Gregory VII ('Hildebrand'), and had maintained a correspondence with William the Conqueror's great archbishop of Canterbury, the ambitious Lanfranc. Murtagh himself was the recipient of letters from Anselm, Lanfranc's successor. It was Anselm, indeed, who in 1096 had consecrated an Irishman, Malchus (Mael Ísu) O Hanvery the first bishop of the Ostmen of Waterford. Contacts such as these had brought home to Murtagh just how out of step with European practice were the Irish Church and Irish secular society. In 1098 he took the decisive step of inviting a Meath bishop, Maelmhuire O Doonan, to be what amounted to Bishop of Killaloe. The translation brought to the king's side an Irishman imbued with the idea of a reform of the Church, and planted him firmly in the heartland of O Brien power. Partly as a result of the Norman conquest of England, lay pilgrimage to Rome had largely dried up—one of the last notables to go had been Murtagh's royal great-uncle Donagh, last of the sons of Brian Bóromha—but coins show that contact continued, while there was in Rome an Irish house with a perhaps characteristic dedication to the Holy Trinity. It was through channels such as these that O Doonan would shortly receive a legatine commission to Munster from Pope Paschal II.

The *Book of Rights* seems to have been drawn up at approximately this time to give the semblance of venerable antiquity and so of legitimacy to O Brien claims to a sovereignty of all Ireland that almost by definition cannot go back beyond Bóromha. Murtagh, however, was not the man to rest content with archaising verbiage however elegant, and a feature of his long reign was the almost monotonous regularity with which he led the Munstermen and their allies on often protracted campaigns which ranged right across Leinster, Connacht and even Ulster. Undoubtedly these wars proved a heavy burden on the Munster economy, and if the booty provided welcome injections of capital the constant blood-letting must in the end have weakened seriously the O Brien position in Thomond vis-a-vis Desmond. The campaigns were mounted, though, with perspicacity as well as pertinacy, and it is typical that in 1100 it had been arranged for a fleet of the Ostmen from Dublin to be cruising off Inishowen as the Munster army prepared to force the lower Erne near Ballyshannon. In the event the land-assault miscarried, and the Dubliners were worsted when attempting to operate independently on their own initiative, but that a rebuff so far from home was not disastrous is in itself a vindication of Murtagh's appreciation of the northern situation. The Tyrone line of the northern O Neill was generally in the ascendancy under the energetic Donal Mac Loughlin, but was preoccupied with its own attempt to impose its authority on the kingdoms of Ulidia east of the Bann. To the south Farney and Oriel were often at loggerheads, and Meath the prey of its own dissensions and of the O Rourke of Breifne. Thus Munster armed intervention might be resented, but could rarely be effectively opposed. Still, too, Murtagh was master of the Shannon, and the Ostmen of Limerick were glad to put at his disposal the ships with which to exploit this advantage.

Early in 1101, though, Murtagh's preoccupation was with the Church, and preparations were made for a council which would bring together at Cashel the clergy and the nobility of Munster and Leinster. This First Synod of Cashel was essentially concerned with ecclesiastical reform, and at first sight the presence of the laity may seem strangely out of place in the context of post-Hildebrandine reformation. The Irish Church, however, was still at a very primitive stage of its development, and Murtagh was realist enough to recognise that large areas of the Church either were controlled by the laity or were incapable of being remodelled without lay co-operation or support. There were after all both Frankish and Anglo-Saxon precedents for a lay presence at a council of this kind, and if Murtagh behaved at Cashel in a manner not a little reminiscent of an emperor Constantine at Nicea, due regard may be thought to have been had to twelfth-century proprieties when O Doonan graced the proceedings as papal legate. Eight principal decrees were promulgated. The first condemned simony, and the second proclaimed ecclesiastical exemption from secular tribute. In Ireland a particular problem had been the quartering of troops on monasteries, and it is significant that the solution which proved in the event most effective was the granting by temporal rulers of individual immunities to an ever widening number of the houses in question. The third decree insisted that ecclesiastical benefices could only be held by clerics, while the fourth attempted to limit if not prohibit overlapping as well as parallel jurisdictions. Both these abuses were peculiarly prevalent in an Ireland which had been passed by where Roman canon law was concerned, and the problem of the coarb or hereditary proprietor of a saint's patrimony was one which lay outside the canonist's experience. Only less critical was another Irish peculiarity, the erenagh, often a layman and married, who occupied church land at a nominal rent and could dispose of it to his heirs on the same terms in perpetuity. The fifth and sixth decrees were more in the European tradition when they sought not very successfully to outlaw clerical concubinage, a problem in Ireland right up until the seventeenth century, and to re-establish rights of sanctuary by remedying some of the more glaring abuses. Finally the seventh decree redefined what in England was to become known as benefit of clergy, the exemption of clerics from secular jurisdiction, extending it in the process to scholar-poets, while the eighth concerned itself very tentatively with an area of the very greatest delicacy involving cleric and layman alike. This was the law of matrimony. Whatever lip-service the Irish Church might have paid to monogamy in principle, it is clear that among the nobility at least traditional Irish law and custom still prevailed. We do not know that any of Brian Bóromha's four spouses in fact predeceased him, and Lanfranc and Anselm in turn had inveighed against Irish propensity to divorce and even promiscuity. For the present, however, the Cashel synodists contented themselves with a condemnation only of unions which on the narrower of the interpretations of the language would be deemed incestuous by almost any right-minded society. The wording of the decrees is at all times remarkably restrained having regard to the extravagance of contemporary denunciations; and concerning the marriage law of the laity there is much to be said for the view that the churchmen, novice if not reluctant canonists, judged it prudent not to jeopardise incipient reform by antagonising these secular forces which the Church would have to enlist if it was to hope to survive. It was in the higher levels of society that matrimonial abuse was most prevalent, and little was to be gained at this stage by bastardising princes and affronting men and women who at worst might be munificent patrons and who were often and not only by their own lights more than just conventionally devout.

At the end of the day Murtagh and O Doonan could sit back and congratulate themselves on a substantial achievement. The banner of reform had been hoisted, and it had not been shot down. That temporal advantage accrued to the monarchy to us may not be obvious, but it is perhaps most clearly seen in an exuberant gesture which set the scene for the proceedings as a whole. Cashel was the old Eoganacht capital of Munster, and had venerable associations with Christian monarchy in days when the Dalcassian kings were still pagan, and Tara a heathen sanctuary. It was a natural focus for resurgent Eoganacht sentiment that was finding a secure base in Desmond, and Murtagh by a master-stroke removed it from the political arena. The seal of O Brien approval of the synod was his gift of the Rock of Cashel to the Irish Church in perpetuity, and the intention may also have included the erection of an ecclesiastical authority in the south of the island which would challenge at least if it did not replace an Armagh choked for more than a century by the domination of the dynasty known as Clann Sinaich. It is to the munificence of Murtagh, then, that we can trace back the origins of the present province of Cashel, and one is left wondering whether an Irish primacy might not have attached in time to the new see had the political cards been stacked differently or there been in the north no Celsus and Malachy.

Murtagh now felt free to turn to more mundane affairs. The Munster and Leinster hosts once more were mustered, and again he led them up the Shannon and into what is now Donegal. The old O Neill fortress at Ailech on Grennan Mountain at the gateway to Inishowen was slighted, and the same fate awaited another of the northern analogues of Cashel of the Kings beside Coleraine. Ulidia east of the Bann was by definition almost well-disposed to the humblers of the O Neills, and Murtagh swung south across Tyrone to rub salt into Mac Loughlin wounds by a ceremonial progress along the old royal road which ran from Navan Fort just outside Armagh to the Hill of Tara. That a patched up truce was made in the following year for twelve months only was due to the efforts of one of the maligned O Sinaich coarbs of Patrick, Donal mac Amalgada, who appears as one of the great peace-makers in

Irish history. It was perhaps on this occasion that the seed was sown among Clann Sinaich of the desirability of Armagh adhering to the reform, though it is worth noting that in 1102 an O Morgair dignitary from Armagh had died at Mungret. The same year there arrived in Irish waters the roving king of Norway, Magnus Olavsson nicknamed 'Barelegs', who had been making a colourful attempt to impose his sovereignty on the descendants of the Norse colonists of the Scottish Isles and Man. Ostmen cities such as Dublin, Waterford and Limerick were of obvious interest, but their integration into the Irish polity seems to have been by now too complete for Magnus to have any real chance of imposing an external allegiance. Murtagh, however, was taking no chances, and the Norwegian king was received at Kincora with every honour. A widower already betrothed to the king of Sweden's daughter, he was ineligible to become Murtagh's son-in-law, but he was accompanied by his thirteen-year-old son Sigurd and a match was soon concluded. It cannot well be a coincidence that the following summer found both kings campaigning in northeast Ireland though the operations appear to have been remarkably ill-coordinated. Donal Mac Loughlin had again attacked Ulidia, but Murtagh's arrival relieved the situation, and the Munster king turned aside to Armagh where he left on the altar a royal O Brien gift of eight ounces of gold before marching southeast into Iveagh. Here the Munster host began to disperse to return home by different routes, and on 5 August 1103 the Leinstermen and a contingent of the Dubliners were unlucky enough to have to face the entire army of the Mac Loughlins and their allies at Mag Coba somewhere north of Newry. The slaughter was immense, and Murtagh himself lost a brother Donagh campaigning on his own account not all that distance to the northeast. Within three weeks Magnus 'Barelegs' himself was dead, axed down near Strangford on 24 August by one of the

Ulidians whose cause he was supposed to be embracing. That in the following year Murtagh seems to have mounted no major offensive outside Munster is scarcely surprising, but such was the resilience of the man and of his resources that in 1105 he is found hosting across Longford and Roscommon as far as Cavan and Meath and even Louth. It is clear though that the spoil on this occasion proved inconsistent with the effort, and it may be thought that the highwater mark of Munster's military greatness was already passed.

In the meantime there had been sensational developments where reform of the Church had been concerned. In 1105 the worthy Donal mac Amalgada had died while absent from Armagh on yet another of his peace-making bids, and his successor as coarb of Patrick was a great-nephew Celsus ('Cellach') whose O Sinaich grandfather, great-grandfather and great-great-grandfather had all in their time enjoyed the coarbship. Celsus, however, was imbued with the spirit of reform, and one of his first acts was to seek priestly ordination. Episcopal consecration would not have been consistent with his principles since there was already in Armagh a relatively obscure cleric tamely performing the spiritual functions of that office. The family connection secured for Celsus general recognition in the north, but it was perhaps inevitable that he should turn towards Munster where secular authority was exhibiting far more foresight in its commitment to reform of the Church. In 1106 he made a circuit of Munster as a coarb of Patrick pledged to reform, and the timely death of the episcopal colleague back in Armagh meant that there was now no canonical obstacle to the heir of Patrick's patrimony receiving appropriate consecration. The consecrator was almost certainly O Doonan whose legatine status there is no reason at all to suppose had lapsed, and we can imagine the joy with which the exile from Meath gave his blessing to the northerner to whom appertained all the prestige of a successor of Patrick. When Celsus returned home, too, it was with the knowledge that reform could be made an attractive proposition to secular as well as religious interests, and that formally at least there was no good political reason why a Donal Mac Loughlin might not become another Murtagh O Brien.

In 1106 or 1107 it was decided to divide the see of Killaloe to take account of political reality. In part as a consequence of a disastrous fire at Kincora, Murtagh had removed his chief residence to Limerick, and the new outlook is seen in the fact that the claims of Mungret, for example, were apparently ignored, and the new seat of the bishop established in what was virtually the Munster capital. O Doonan, who may well have been beginning to fail, was left at Killaloe, and the first of the bishops of Limerick was a certain Gillebert ('Gilla Easpuig'). Limerick was a town of the Ostmen, but consecration was not sought from Canterbury, though as a matter of courtesy Anselm was kept in the picture by a letter accompanied by a gift of pearls. Gillebert was an articulate as well as ardent reformer, a David to O Doonan's Saul, and within a year or so of his consecration he had put out a short but convincing treatise with the self-explanatory title *De Statu Ecclesiae* ('On the State of the Church'). This not merely expounded the conventional European hierarchy, but could assume that there were some at least in secular society who would be aware that it too was very different from that which obtained elsewhere in Western Europe. Thus there were now concentrated in Munster three of the outstanding figures in the Irish reform movement, the venerable O Doonan, the no less enlightened O Hanvery at Waterford, and the eloquent Gillebert. Most of Leinster was at worst neutral, and Celsus promised to be in a position to set in order the affairs of most of Ulster. Probably the most urgent problems were presented by Dublin and by Connacht. At the former, Samuel O Hanley was playing the metropolitan to the discomfort of all parties, and not least his 1096 consecrator Anselm of Canterbury. It says much for the wisdom of the reformers that they seem to have thought it best to ignore Dublin rather than force Samuel, a kinsman of his predecessor, into a position where reconciliation with Canterbury could lead to a revival of English ambition. Connacht, however, was remote and isolated, and in 1108 Celsus made a circuit of the province and was everywhere acknowledged. It was to be the same in 1110 when he progressed around Meath. Prestige attached to the reform in the person of Patrick's successor, but it remained a serious flaw that its principal lay proponent and protector still was thwarted of the High Kingship so obviously dear to his heart. In 1109 Celsus had again made peace between Murtagh and Donal Mac Loughlin for a year, but the death of Donal O'Brien's wife in 1110 removed one of the last restraints on the two men. Ominously, too, Donal was now hosting further afield, and he seems to have drowned his sorrow in a foray into Connacht from which the spectacular booty was in marked contrast to the meagre spoils which had come Murtagh's way when he had hosted into the north of Breifne the previous year.

Donal, however, did ever lack the imperial touch, and in 1111 Murtagh may be said to have regained the propaganda initiative when there assembled, at a place called variously Fiad Mac nAengusa and Raith Bresail between Thurles and Templemore, a major synod of the Irish Church. Appointed papal legate in place of the retiring O Doonan was Gillebert, though it is interesting that the *Annals of Inisfallen*, perhaps because being composed at this period at Killaloe, remark the former's presence and ignore the latter's. If a seventeenth-century transcript of the decree establishing a formal hierarchy is to be trusted, the order of precedence among the signatories was 1) Gillebert as papal legate, 2) Celsus as coarb of Patrick and primate, and 3)

Malchus O Hanvery as archbishop of Cashel. The name of O Doonan figured only among those of the twenty-three bishops without legatine or metropolitan status. Ulster was given sees at Armagh, Ardstraw, Clogher, Connor, Down and Raphoe; Meath at Clonard and Duleek; Connacht at Ardagh, Clonfert, Cong, Killala and Tuam. In the southern province Munster was assigned sees at Cashel, the future Ardfert, Cork, Emly, Killaloe, Limerick and Lismore/Waterford; Leinster receiving Ferns, Glendaloch, Kildare, Kilkenny and Leighlin. Over Dublin a veil was discreetly drawn, the consequence probably of O Hanley's continuing intransigence. The total of sees envisaged was thus 26, a remarkable correspondence with the position today after quite a number of both new creations and amalgamations. What is not perhaps sufficiently realised is that the number by Western European standards was quite extravagantly large. Contemporary England for example, where the population was very considerably greater, had to make do with fewer than half the number of sees. The clue to the disparity may be found in the number of 'bishops' reputed to have attended the synod, 'a fair fifty' according to the *Annals of Inisfallen*, 'fifty or a little more' according to the *Annals of Ulster*, 58 if we are to believe the *Annals of Tigernach*. In the Ireland which had been shattered by the Norse invasions and their aftermath, a hundred or so petty kingdoms each had striven to have as a status symbol its own favoured monastery, and each of these houses in its turn would aspire to have within the community someone in bishop's orders. The reformers' thankless task was to try to prune back this too luxuriant sprouting of prestigious episcopacy, and the reduction to 26 in itself must rank as a very real achievement. As it was, this inheritance of superfluity was to cost the Irish Church dear throughout the middle ages, and its effects were to be felt indeed as late as the sixteenth and seventeenth centuries. The new sees, often grossly under-endowed and so only marginally viable from their inception, were vulnerable at the best of times to further lay encroachment on their lands, and one of the problems confronting the Protestant reformers would be the difficulty of attracting administrative talent to further impoverished cathedrals where the precarious income of the episcopal incumbent might well be less than that afforded by a secure and comfortable English living.

At this synod generally today known as that of Ráith Bresail there were also present very large numbers of the lower clergy, and contemporary estimates of three or four hundred are unlikely to be inflated. It was particularly desirable that the attendance should be representative when the decisions arrived at could materially affect the prosperity of so many. Emly, for example, was relatively fortunate to be awarded one of the new sees, but the need adequately to endow Cashel meant that a limit was effectively set to her hopes of future expansion. In other cases a compromise was arrived at by linking formally a major monastery with a novel conurbation, the association of Lismore with Waterford being a case in point. The claims of other houses might be ignored or disallowed, and the case of Clonmacnois is sufficient to show that this was not always because the house in question was in decline. There can be little doubt, too, that secular interests still reared their head, and there does seem to be some congruity between the pattern of the new episcopate and the realities of political power. Murtagh himself was prominent at the synod, and again there was a substantial attendance of prominent laymen. The bishops' other main concern appears to have been the old question of the Church's immunity from tribute and taxation, and the laymen present would have been those with a particular interest in the eventual outcome. It would be wrong, though, to end on a note implying pure expediency. The presence in one and the same place of so many of the more influential of the clergy and of the laity of Ireland gives Raith Bresail a character all of its own. If, too, it afforded the preacher a unique pulpit from which to inveigh against evils that too often seem irrelevant to modern living, it is no less true that it constituted a symbol of national unity in a fratricidal age, and even if it were no more than this, it would still represent a very real O Brien triumph of the same order as Clontarf a century earlier.

Raith Bresail gave the Irish Church a recognisable hierarchy on the European model. It remained for the reformers to give this hierarchy teeth, and the next generation saw a great deal of patient and unspectacular work in building up a diocesan structure in the face of prejudice and vested interest. For nearly a generation Gillebert as papal legate had a general oversight of the developments, but the *Annals of Inisfallen* are curiously reticent, a consequence perhaps of Killaloe's grievance at the erection of his see. As Ireland sank, too, into an orgy of internecine conflict the task of the reformers became more and more difficult and less and less likely to achieve major break-throughs. Flexibility had of necessity to be the order of the day, and within months of Raith Bresail a more local but still critical synod was held at Uisneach, the modern Ushnagh Hill, in Meath. The province had fallen on evil days, and Raith Bresail's decisions for the episcopate reflected neither political nor ecclesiastical reality. In the Meath orbit lay one of the greatest of all the monasteries of Ireland, Clonmacnois, and it was one which presented the reform with special problems. Few religious houses stood less in need of moral reformation. The abbacy had not been allowed to become the prerogative of a single family or of royal competition, and the life of the monks seems to have been as regular as their tradition of learning impeccable. With late eleventh and early twelfth-century Clonmacnois there are associated such major works of Irish scholarship as the *Chronicon Scotorum* composed by the actual abbot in attendance at Uisneach, Gilla Crist

O Malone, the slightly earlier *Lebor na hUidre* ('Book of the Dun Cow') compiled by Maelmhuire Mac Kelleher, and the so-called *Annals of Tigernach* begun by the eponymous Tigernach O Beirne of the founder's kin. Any assault on so respectable and even edifying an institution needed to be carried out with discretion, and particularly when Gilla Crist was capable of articulate resistance to novelty. Raith Bresail had given Meath sees in Clonard and Duleek; Uisneach drew the line of partition further west, gave Clonmacnois the western diocese and made Clonard the seat of the bishop of east Meath, so that Duleek was the sufferer under the new arrangement which does seem to have been dictated by political reality if we are to judge from the failure of a later attempt to implement the original intention of Raith Bresail.

In the meantime Murtagh had been addressing himself to secular concerns. A cousin's child, Brian, appears to have been acting as a focus of discontent within Thomond, and as a result of some action taken against him went to the north of Ireland, and presumably to the court of Murtagh's old rival Donal Mac Loughlin. Nearer still to the king, a restless nephew, Donal, likewise decamped but roved even further afield, and for a time succeeded in having himself accepted as king of at least some of the Norse of the Scottish Isles. The departures seem to have cleared the air, and from Michaelmas until Christmas Murtagh was absent from Munster on a protracted visit to his Dublin allies. War was in the offing everywhere in Ireland, and the news from the north was of a spirited foray by the Ulidians around Lough Neagh to desecrate a ceremonial grove of the O Neills at Tullahogue. Retaliation was meted out not by the ageing Donal Mac Loughlin but by his son Niall, though events in the years that followed showed that the father still was capable of hosting at his army's head. In 1112, indeed, Donal was campaigning in person as far as the hinterland of Dublin. The following year there was a direct confrontation of the O Briens and O Neills when Murtagh marched north to Armagh and into Iveagh to bring relief to the hardpressed Ulidians. That a truce was arranged between the two great rivals once again was due to the initiative of Celsus, and for the present it must have seemed that neither side was in a position to inflict a mortal wound upon the other.

In 1114 the uneasy balance of power was utterly destroyed when an illness, probably some sort of stroke, left Murtagh totally incapacitated. His brother Dermot invaded the sickroom to proclaim his usurpation, and the invalid was bundled out of Limerick and interned at Killaloe, the monastery rather than the old palace of Kincora being a more likely choice of place of confinement for an old king written off as on the point of death. Donal Mac Loughlin's intelligence appears to have been good, and within weeks the northern hosts with Connacht allies were invading Munster, and winning a major victory at Corofin in the heart of what is now Co. Clare. Operations appear to have been conducted on both sides with unusual savagery, but eventually some sort of truce was made. Donal's troubles in Ulster had not been ended by a submission of the Ulidians earlier in the year, and he too appears to have had dynastic problems that concerned the succession and which resulted in the murder of his son and designated heir. With his departure northwards the Munstermen had time to ponder the conduct of Dermot, and we will probably not be far wrong if we imagine that the aged O Doonan lent his moral support to a coup which resulted in Murtagh's return to power early in 1115. Claims of old friendship apart, Europeanising trends inextricably bound up with the new movement for reform demanded that the principles of legitimacy be publicly vindicated, and the only concession made to Irish traditions which had sanctioned Dermot's succession during the king's incapacity was the sparing of the culprit's life. After a period of imprisonment he was released having first sworn the most solemn of oaths that there would be no repetition of the treachery. In the meantime Murtagh's son Donal was leading the Ostmen of Dublin to a significant victory over the Leinstermen, and to mark his recovery Murtagh hosted in person across Ossory and north Leinster as far as Brega. The achievement is not diminished by the reflection that Murtagh knew that his left flank was secure while Connacht remained in confusion following a domestic conspiracy which had left for dead the young Turlough O Connor. Among the subsequent victims of the disorder was at least one potential quisling where Murtagh was concerned, the adventurous Donal who earlier had been kinging it among the turbulent Norsemen of the Scottish Isles.

Murtagh's restoration did not last long. Turlough O Connor made a dramatic recovery from his wounds, and proclaimed it to the world by a hosting into Thomond which brought him to the gates of Limerick. Famine stalked the whole island, but still the princes and their captains warred. Murtagh for his part mounted in 1116 yet another invasion of Leinster which seems largely to have miscarried, while the excesses of the troops generally such a good friend to the Church reformers and who was added to the people's misery. It is probably not altogether a coincidence that Celsus chose this moment for a pastoral visitation of Connacht. He may well have wished to see if he could use his good offices politically in a bid to take some of the pressure off the king of Munster who had been now so obviously failing. The débâcle in Leinster gave Dermot O Brien a new opportunity for mischief, and once more Murtagh was declared to be deposed. The victim of this fraternal treachery took refuge in Limerick, and it can have been no more than a crumb of comfort that self-interest led to his being joined there by the Brian whom he had virtually driven into exile some five years before. In

Limerick the old king was probably safe enough. He had ever been a good friend to the Ostmen, and Bishop Gillebert was his protégé. His spirit, however, was broken, and a dear sister was dying if not already dead. The moment had come for abdication. His friends he could no longer provide for, and it is probably no coincidence that we find the aged and venerable O Doonan dying the very next year not in Thomond but at Clonard. The king himself chose to go into exile at Lismore, and it is probably the same wind of change that explains why he had as his bishop there another old friend from the days of the synods of Cashel and Raith Bresail, Malchus O Hanvery, who seems to have renounced the metropolitan dignity to die as simple bishop of Waterford in 1135. The royal exile, however, did not long enjoy his ghostly consolations. The year 1117 was given up to war in the north where the O Neills fought among themselves for Inishowen, in Meath where the O Melaghlin king was worsted by an alliance between the Dubliners and the Leinstermen, and the community at Kells massacred by O Beirne raiders from Roscommon, and in Thomond where Brian O Brien brought in troops from Connacht and scored a notable victory over those Dalcassians who had declared for Dermot and were led by his son Turlough. Early in 1118, though, Dermot died at Cork, allegedly penitent and if so with good cause, and Murtagh's own not altogether disinterested paladin Brian was killed in battle when attempting to impose his own particular version of O Brien overlordship on a Desmond where the Mac Carthys had sniffed prospects of profit in Thomond's discomfiture. Brian had been styled by the chroniclers 'royal heir' of Munster, and one of the minor mysteries is what had become of Murtagh's own sons. Donal appears to vanish from history after his defeat of the Leinstermen in 1115, while Mahon is known only from a record of his death at Lismore in 1129. Was he perhaps automatically debarred by debility or deformity from the royal succession? Dermot's sons Conor and Turlough, on the other hand, were well able to look after their own interests, and without external interference might soon have brought back Desmond to a respectful dependence. It was a state of affairs that Turlough O Connor in Connacht was not prepared to allow to develop, and Murtagh's exile at Lismore was abruptly ended when there arrived an offer from Turlough to reinstate him. With pathetic trust in Turlough's good faith, Murtagh joined a great hosting of the men of Connacht and their allies. Kincora was finally and irretrievably slighted, the stone and timbers being cast into the Shannon, before Murtagh himself was the subject of one final humiliation. His presence had sufficed to divide the O Briens, and Turlough was master of Munster. The setting sun could serve no further purpose, and the very limited future now envisaged for the O Briens lay with younger men. Munster was to be partitioned between a Desmond under the Mac Carthys and a Thomond in turn divided between Dermot's sons, Conor and Turlough. A few months later Murtagh was dead, his last days spent in bitter impotence as a virtual hostage at Killaloe.

The sees of twelfth-century Ireland

RAPHOE   **Derry**   CONNOR

Ardstraw   **DOWN**

CLOGHER   **ARMAGH   Dromore**

MAGHERA

KILLALA

ACHONRY   KILMORE

MAYO   ELPHIN   ARDAGH

Cong   **TUAM**   KELLS

Clonmacnois   DULEEK

Annaghdown
CLONFERT   **DUBLIN**

KILMACDUAGH   CLONARD   KILDARE

GLENDALOCH
KILLALOE   ROSCREA   LEIGHLIN

KILKENNY

SCATTERY   LIMERICK   **CASHEL**   FERNS

EMLY   **Ardmore**

CLOYNE   LISMORE   WATERFORD

ARDFERT

CORK

ROSS   **ARMAGH**   Metropolitan see recognized at Synod of Kells
ACHONRY   Suffragan see recognized at Synod of Kells
Annaghdown   Suffragan see subsequent to Synod of Kells
Ardstraw   Suffragan see not surviving Synod of Kells

22

2 Connacht's Heyday

TURLOUGH O CONNOR, the architect of the overthrow of O Brien supremacy in Munster and so of Dalcassian aspirations to the High Kingship, was a man still in his twenties. He had been born c. 1088, and was a child of four when his father was trapped and blinded by the O Flahertys from Connemara. Five years later his older brother Tadhg met a violent death, and the young prince grew up in a Connacht dominated by the O Rourkes of Breifne. O Rourke power, however, was already on the wane, partly as a consequence of the growing power of the Mac Loughlins further to the north, and it was in 1114, when Donal Mac Loughlin hosted into Munster, that Turlough emerged overnight as one of the protagonists in the affairs of Ireland as a whole. A son-in-law of Donal's he still could take an independent line, and it is likely that his defection from the Ulster host was an important factor in Donal's decision to withdraw. We can well imagine that Turlough was reluctant to see a failing O Brien replaced by a Mac Loughlin likely to turn out to be 'king stork' in the place of 'king log'. Donal, however, was a septuagenarian, and his attempts to curb the growing power of Connacht proved quite ineffective. In 1119 Turlough had stationed himself with a fleet at Killaloe, a warning to Thomond that O Connor considered himself the master of Munster, and Donal for his part suffered a severe setback to his hopes when his son Niall was killed while attempting to assert Mac Loughlin authority over the area of Donegal around

Raphoe. In the following year there was an overt confrontation of the two protagonists when Donal brought the northern host to Athlone, but a truce was negotiated between the old king and his ambitious son-in-law. We may perhaps see in this the hand of Celsus who the same year made a circuit of Munster, but Turlough clearly regarded the peace as no more than a breathing-space. The building of a bridge across the Shannon at Athlone should have been a warning to the whole island that for the future O Connor ambitions would not be confined to Connacht.

Early in 1121 Donal Mac Loughlin died at Derry, and Turlough judged rightly that a major campaign in Munster could now be mounted without fear of northern intervention. Desmond suffered terribly, and more than seventy churches were burned, including the venerable monastery of Lismore. It was small comfort for the victims that the fatal casualties inflicted on the invaders included sub-kings from Connemara and from the mearing of Clare and Galway. Turlough wintered at Birr, and from there proclaimed once more the definitive partitioning of Munster between an O Brien Thomond and a Mac Carthy Desmond. The death of his wife Mór meant that he would have a new freedom of action where the north was concerned, though for the present her brother Conor was preoccupied with the age-old struggle to bring to heel Ulidia where he was able to host as far as Kilroot in Antrim. Turlough himself hosted north-eastwards to the vicinity of Dunboyne where he received the formal submission of the Dubliners who hitherto had belonged as a rule to the Munster orbit. Leinster also made formal submission, and a marriage to Tailtiu, an O Melaghlin princess, meant that Turlough could be represented as having authority over four of the historic 'fifths' of Ireland. The island, however, was far from being at peace. There was internal strife in Meath and Ossory, a royal heir slain in Donegal, and in Thomond a sacrilegious attack on the abbot of Emly at the hands of an apostate cleric. Even in the Church the old order died hard. Meanwhile resentment at Connacht's novel suzerainty was growing apace, and in 1123 Cormac Mac Carthy displaced his brother Tadhg, who had been struck down by a fatal disease, and to some extent mastermined a general revolt which spread from Munster to Leinster, Meath and Breifne. Turlough's reply was to bring his fleet to Limerick, and to devastate parts of Thomond and of Desmond with complete ruthlessness. Most of the city of Limerick was burnt down, and such fear was instilled into Desmond that Cormac was faced with mutiny when he attempted to take his army into the Midlands to succour the rebels there who had been heavily defeated by Turlough near Granard. In the end Cormac marched north with only part of his forces, and the plan seems to have been that the four armies together would invade north Connacht to relieve the pressure on Munster. Turlough's reply was to put to death the Munster hostages who included Cormac's own son Malachy, and to interpose his own army between the allies and their prey by a lightning march to Athlone. The coalition broke up, and Turlough resumed his position at Limerick.

In 1125 Turlough addressed himself to Meath where he deposed his father-in-law and gave most of the territory to rival lines of the O Melaghlin house but part to Tighernan O Rourke who would appear to have switched Breifne back to its more traditional alignment. The Dubliners seem to have been made subordinate to Leinster for a few months before Turlough's own son Conor was put over them, but once more Munster boiled over in revolt and the men of Meath broke down the Shannon bridges at Athlone and above Banagher. The O Briens were prominent in the early stages of the rebellion, but Cormac Mac Carthy emerged as the real leader. When Turlough in 1126 intervened in the Leinster succession to procure the acceptance of Dermot Mac Murrough, Cormac again marched north-eastwards but was routed on the borders of Ossory and pursued as far as Glanmire in what is now Co. Cork. Turlough then turned back and devastated Donegal as far as Raphoe in reprisal for an attack on north Connacht. In 1127 he hosted into Munster as far as Cork, turned into Ossory and finally rounded on Dermot Mac Murrough and deposed him in favour of Conor already ruling in Dublin. In theory at least rebellious Munster was now hemmed in by an O Connor-ruled power-block comprising the whole of Connacht and the whole of modern Leinster south of the Boyne. In Ulster there was internecine war, and for thirteen months Celsus was absent from Armagh attempting to bring the Irish laity to their senses. His own kin were not immune to violence within Armagh itself, but the moral degradation of the country was perhaps best seen in 1128 when Tighernan O Rourke ambushed the archbishop and slew a young cleric under the primate's own eyes.

The scapegoat for Munster's misfortunes was Cormac Mac Carthy who in 1127 followed Murtagh O Brien's example, abdicated and entered the monastery at Lismore. Turlough partitioned Desmond into three, but opposition to him in the rest of Ireland was steadily mounting even if for the moment muted. His favoured religious house was Clonmacnois where we have seen that the reform had been received with less than enthusiasm, and the reformers in the Church seem to have played a considerable part in building up a coalition which clipped Turlough's wings if it did not destroy him. The O Brien princes came to Lismore and buried the hatchet where the Mac Carthys were concerned by urging Cormac to resume his kingship of Desmond. The aged Malchus O Hanvery gave the same counsel, and so did the royal penitent's spiritual director, Malachy O Morgair ('Mael Moedoc'), already a favoured son of the reform at Armagh, who was at Lismore as an exile from his abbey at Bangor and see of Connor – shades of the father who had died at Mungret in 1102. Cormac allowed himself to be persuaded, and returned in triumph to his own. His brother Donagh and a few others fled to Turlough where they played the quisling with remarkably little success, and they were joined from Leinster and Dublin by Turlough's son Conor. The deposed puppet prince cannot have been more than a boy, and even an experienced statesman would have found it hard to ride out the storm that was gathering in the territories that had tasted for the first time Connacht overlordship. Nor were matters helped at this time by the death of Tailtiu, Turlough's most obvious channel of influence where Meath was concerned.

Tighernan O Rourke, however, could be relied on to cover the Upper Shannon, and so Turlough gathered his fleet below Limerick, his intention being to bring first to heel the O Briens. There was much devastation, but in the end a Munster fleet entered Lough Derg, and the O Connor stranglehold on the Lower Shannon was broken. The good offices of Celsus were called into play, and Turlough agreed to a year's truce which for Cormac Mac Carthy and Conor O Brien amounted to a very solid victory. The pressure at last was off, and they could consolidate their positions in Desmond and Thomond respectively. Turlough consoled himself by a massive hosting into Leinster and up the Wicklow coast to Dublin which was without enduring result, and in his absence Tighernan O Rourke suffered a sharp defeat at the hands of Conor Mac Loughlin who followed up this success with campaigns further east and in Ulidia. Ulster was once more an all-Ireland power which Turlough could not afford to leave out of his reckoning, though it was unfortunate that Conor within months should have sullied his good name by a sack of Trim which did not spare the churches.

The following year (1129) saw the death of Celsus at Ardpatrick while on yet another visit to Munster. At his own request he was buried at Lismore. The last years of his pontificate had brought him much sadness, but he had obtained one notable success. It will be remembered that the synods of Cashel and of Raith Bresail had papered over the problem at Dublin posed by the intransigence of the Canterbury-consecrated Samuel O Hanley. In 1121 Samuel had died, and one Gregory ('Greine' or 'Grenne') received episcopal consecration at Canterbury. Celsus for his part seems to have been able to prevent him exercising jurisdiction – the Irish annalists even imply somewhat improbably that he himself held Dublin in plurality – and Ralph d'Escures showed himself no Anselm, let alone Lanfranc. Gregory renounced his Canterbury allegiance, accepted Celsus as metropolitan, and in 1152 would receive as his reward the status after which Samuel had hungered in vain. In 1129, however, the outlook for the reform must have seemed dubious as well as dismal. Malchus at Waterford was an old man, and Gillebert at Limerick ruled an impoverished and war-torn diocese. It is clear, too, that Celsus' repeated absences from Armagh had weakened the cause of reform in the northern province, while Malachy's long exile in Lismore may well have reflected lack of sympathy if not downright hostility on the part of the O Neill monarchy. Celsus' immediate successor as coarb of Patrick, Maurice ('Murtagh'), was not only a layman, and from the notorious Clann Sinaich, but positively spurned episcopal consecration. When he died in 1135 the coarbship passed back to Celsus' brother, Nigel ('Niall'), who soon came into head-on collision with the reform. Before that, however, the reformers had ensured the archiepiscopal succession by insisting that the reluctant and exiled Malachy accept translation to Armagh – he was already, of course, in episcopal orders. In 1133 Maurice had processed around the north as coarb, and in 1134 Malachy retorted with a Patrician circuit of Munster which must have brought him useful revenues as well as a measure of prestige. When Niall succeeded as coarb in the following year, Malachy realised that the time had come to advance north and challenge the Clann Sinaich. By 1137 Nigel had had to vacate Armagh, and Malachy could make an eirenic proposal which would cut the ground from under the feet of any who might suggest that self-interest lay behind his advocacy of primatial status for Armagh, and which no less effectively disposed of any objection that he himself was *persona non grata* where any or all of the Mac Loughlins were concerned. This was the suggestion that he should lay down the archbishopric of Armagh in favour of the abbot of Derry, Gelasius Mac Rory ('Gilla Mac Liac'), a northerner sympathetic to reform but politically uncompromised, while Malachy would withdraw to Bangor and confine the exercise of his episcopal functions to the see of Down. Gelasius' task as primate and coarb would be to conciliate, but it would be from a position of strength, Malachy's own brother Christian ('Gilla Crist') having been consecrated in 1135 to the see of Clogher to which were transferred for the next half-century or so at Armagh's expense, the lands in Louth that were to have constituted the abortive see of Duleek. There was an element of secular politics in all this, a building-up as it were of the position of Donagh O Carroll, the king of Oriel, as some sort of counterpoise to Mac Loughlin dominance of the northern scene. Malachy for his part was free to concentrate on pastoral work in his own diocese and on maintaining and extending a quite extraordinary range of contacts with churchmen throughout Ireland and significant new developments elsewhere in western Europe. It was indicative of the careful planning and essential soundness of the new phase of the reform that Christian's death in 1138 did not disrupt the programme. Late in 1139 Malachy left Ireland for Rome.

Secular affairs during this decade were less edifying. In 1130 and 1131 Connacht fleets ravaged the coastline of Desmond, and in the latter year Turlough brought an army into West Limerick, confident apparently that the palisaded earthwork or 'castle' he had thrown up at Athlone would secure his newly repaired bridge and so guard his rear. Conor O Brien replied by an abortive raid into Westmeath which in the event never swung west across the Shannon. In the meantime Conor Mac Loughlin was inflicting yet another crushing defeat upon the Ulidians, an essential preliminary to any intervention further to the south. In 1131 this occurred, and the O Neill host crossed the Erne near Ballyshannon and came as far as the vicinity of Boyle. Its rearguard, however, was mauled by an élite corps of Connachtmen, and an accommodation arrived at whereby the Ulster army would withdraw. The Ulidian contingents fell in with Tighernan O Rourke's men from Breifne who had been profiting by their absence to plunder in east Ulster, and in the ensuing battle the Ulidians were again worsted. Cormac Mac Carthy and Conor O Brien were no more fortunate. They crossed the Shannon above Limerick and attempted to invade Connacht by way of Clare which vainly sought to remain neutral. Tempers flared, and Conor narrowly escaped assassination at the hands of one of the Clare sub-kings who was promptly executed. In the end nothing was achieved beyond the destruction of much Munster property. For all this, the repulse of the Munstermen is the highwater mark of Turlough's career. In 1132 Conor Mac Loughlin hosted as far as Ardee, and Tighernan O Rourke again switched his allegiance away from Connacht. Not much is made in the annals of this defection, but it was to be more momentous for Ireland than the far more sensational incident in the same year when Dermot Mac Murrough intervened to try and impose a kinswoman on the great convent at Kildare, and the rival abbess was bedded with a common soldier to render her unfit to continue in office. In 1133 a combined army from Desmond and Thomond plundered in Connacht as far as Mayo, and in Meath and Leinster there was much destruction of life and property as second-rank Irish kings like Donagh O Carroll and Dermot Mac Murrough jockeyed for position in the Dublin hinterland. Matters were not helped by a murrain or cattle-pest of proportions unknown for centuries. In 1134 there was civil war in the north-west of the island and in Offaly, and heavy fighting as Dermot Mac Murrough attempted to impose his will on Ossory and on the Ostmen of Waterford. The Munster alliance fell apart, and an O Brien prince and his son were slain by the men of Desmond. In 1135 six named Irish sub-kings are recorded in the *Annals of Loch Cé* as meeting violent deaths. Monasteries burned included those at Derry, Maghera, Clonard and Kells. In a battle at Clonkeen in Tipperary there was a bloody victory of the men of Thomond over those of Desmond, and the dedication of Cormac's Chapel on the Rock of Cashel, that monument to Mac Carthy piety, shines out as a truly good deed in a naughty world. It is an indication of Turlough's difficulties at home that he was unable to turn all this dissension to his own profit, and in fact he was glad in 1134 to conclude another year's truce with Munster. In 1136 there was a dangerous conspiracy within his own kin, the position being saved only by the loyalty of his son Conor who led the family retainers to victory over the dissident O Connors and their allies from elsewhere in Connacht. It was essential for Turlough's prestige that he should once again play a dominant role in Irish affairs, and in 1138 he did succeed once more in attracting support from Tighernan O Rourke in Breifne and from Donagh O Carroll in Oriel. For the moment, but only for the moment, O Neill power was in eclipse as a consequence of Conor's assassination at an assembly in Donegal, and so the sub-kings of the Ulster mearing would be less inhibited in seeking allies to the west. It would not be long until the O Neills of the north again would be united behind the young but resolute Murtagh Mac Loughlin, the murdered king's grandson.

By 1140 it was clear that Turlough could not command obedience from his theoretical satellites. O Rourke was again transferring his allegiance, and in the south-east Mac Murrough was pursuing an increasingly independent line which in 1141 culminated in a massacre of the royal family of north Leinster and of their more prominent supporters. Meath as usual was in turmoil. Turlough hosted into Leinster yet again, and Dermot made nominal submission so that it was on paper a formidable coalition of all the forces of Connacht, Meath and Leinster that was now drawn up to intervene in Munster. Conor O Brien had died, and his brother Turlough's claim to be king of Munster as well as of Thomond was challenged by Cormac Mac Carthy. A battle near O'Brien's Bridge favoured Cormac, but at Waterford the Desmond champion was taken prisoner and handed over to Turlough O Brien The Connacht army was unable to intervene with any real effect, and Turlough O Connor once again had disappointed his own. In 1143 Cormac Mac Carthy died in captivity at Lough Gur, his son Donagh dying likewise a prisoner the following year. Turlough O Brien thus was free to mount a spectacular raid into Connacht which cut down a sacred tree at Roevehagh by the Mayo mearing. A conspiracy was formed around Rory O Connor who was promptly arrested by his father who also took into custody the O Melaghlin king of Meath. No fewer than twelve bishops are supposed to have petitioned successfully for the prisoners' release, but Turlough could not be dissuaded from setting his own son Conor over Meath. In 1144 after a reign of only six months this Conor was assassinated, his brother Tadhg apparently dying a natural death the self-same year. The north seems to have been generally quiet following a revolt of Donegal from O Neill overlordship in 1143, but in 1145 the midlands were torn by war with Meath attacking Leinster and Oriel and inflicting a heavy defeat upon Breifne. Again we see Turlough O Connor unable to extract real advantage from the situation and this despite the fact that in 1144 he had been able to secure his right flank by concluding a solemn peace with the O Briens at Terryglass, neutral ground in that it was a Leinster house on Munster soil looking across Lough Derg to Connacht. Turlough O Brien for his part had his difficulties, and had once more to arrest his own brother Tadhg, but an ominous development where O Connor was concerned was the decision of the peoples along the left bank of the Shannon from Lough Derg to Lough Ree to join with Meath in accepting O Brien overlordship. In 1145 or 1146 Turlough O Connor attempted to bring them back to their old dependence, but a battle at Athlone on the bridge itself resulted in heavy casualties for Connacht. Tighernan O Rourke proved no less recalcitrant, and in 1146 actually burnt some Connacht ships near Athlone where in the following year Turlough O Connor's own son Donal was the victim of a third humiliating reverse. Further to the east there was war between the Dubliners and Brega which resulted in the discomfiture of the former, but more and more thinking men's eyes were fixed on the north where Murtagh Mac Loughlin was slowly consolidating his hold on Ulster.

It is no coincidence that the secular power was ignored by the Church when in 1148 a fairly representative synod met at Inis Patraic, a small island off Skerries. There was no one power in Ireland capable of giving decisive backing to a reform movement, and of the five most powerful men in Ireland, Turlough O Connor, Murtagh Mac Loughlin, Turlough O Brien, Dermot Mac Murrough and Tighernan O Rourke, O Connor was at best lukewarm to reform to judge from his patronage of Clonmacnois, while Mac Murrough and O Rourke were men whose crimes against religion could not quite be obliterated by intermittent expiatory munificence. Essentially the fifteen bishops and two hundred lesser clergy were there to hear a report on progress by Malachy, and having heard this to endorse a new approach to Rome for the final seal of papal approval on all that had been done. In 1139 Malachy had set out to pay what could be termed the first *ad limina* visit to Rome of an Irish bishop, and Pope Innocent II received him with evident kindness. It is likely that there was mutual frankness with the Irishman concealing nothing where the state of the lesser clergy and of the laity was under review. Malachy's own first-hand experiences of the opposition of coarb and erenagh and of the sheer ignorance of the common people would have been an argument however unintentional on the side of caution, and his request for *pallia* to be sent to Armagh and to Cashel as visible marks of papal approval of their metropolitan status was gently refused. The time was not yet ripe, and Malachy was told to return to Ireland, to continue the good work, and in due course to make a formal application with specific synodal backing. Papal approval was given, though, for the erection of the two provinces, and for the shape of the reconstituted hierarchy, and it is unlikely that Canterbury here made any effective representations, although Theobald the English primate had recently consecrated a bishop Patrick for Limerick to replace the failing Gillebert, and he himself had just been in Rome. The English nominee, apparently an Irishman, appears in no Irish record, and the probability is that he never gained possession of his see which was ruled by an Irish-consecrated Ostman by the name of Erolf. Gillebert had also asked to be relieved of his legatine appointment, and this the Pope conferred on Malachy, so that it was as papal legate that the Bishop of Down would preside in 1148 at Inis Patraic. His own expressed wish to Innocent II was that he might not return to Ireland but go to Clairvaux and there receive the Cistercian habit from Bernard with whom he had become intimate on his way to Rome, but this boon was refused. The Pope realised that a man so enthusiastic for the regular life might be invaluable for bringing Ireland into conformity with the mainstream of Western European monasticism, and there was the further question of the equal admiration which Malachy had for Gervaise and his Arroaisian reformed Augustinian canons whose rule proved well adapted to the peculiar demands of the Irish situation where the chapters of some of the new cathedrals were concerned.

On his way back to Ireland, Malachy had again visited Clairvaux, and left there some of his companions to be trained in Cistercian ways by Bernard himself. In 1141 they returned to Ireland in company with some of the French monks, and shortly afterwards they were granted land near Drogheda by Donagh O Carroll, and began the construction of Mellifont Abbey. They were not the only monks of foreign formation to labour in Ireland during this decade. Savigny had houses in Down and at Dublin which in time aggregated to the Cistercian rule, and it has been suggested that there were other Benedictine foundations, from Thiron, underlying two future Cistercian houses in Munster, and even that there was a Cluniac house at Athlone. The truth is that Malachy and some of the temporal princes were 'taking Ireland into Europe' for all they were worth, and help from any quarter was unlikely to be refused. If, too, the numismatists are right who opine that it was about this time that coins of a fabric otherwise peculiar to contemporary Germany began to be struck at Clonmacnois, Dublin and possibly Ferns, it would fit in well with the view that German influences can be detected in Cormac's Chapel at Cashel where there does seem to have been a Benedictine house before 1150. A kinsman of Cormac's, Gilla Crist Mac Carthy, was, as it happens, abbot of Regensburg at precisely this period, and is believed to have visited Ireland. Mellifont, however, was undoubtedly the most influential of all the new monastic foundations, and this despite clashes of temperament between the Irish and French monks. Most prominent among the former was Christian ('Gilla Crist') O Conarchy who was to be consecrated to the see of Lismore in 1151 and later to serve as papal legate. Within a decade or so of the foundation of Mellifont, Irish Cistercians were to occupy three Irish sees (Lismore, Clonfert and Kildare), and Mellifont to have made seven foundations, only one abortive. There is a danger, though, that we stress unduly the exceptionally well-documented triumph of the 'white monks'. Malachy's report to the synod of Inis Patraic must have covered in detail an even more substantial achievement, the country's essential acceptance of the Raith Bresail hierarchy, and the conversion to its endowment of a very considerable proportion – though by no means the totality – of the patrimonies of the old monastic Church.

It was the view of the reformers that Rome could and should grant the *pallia* refused in 1140, and Malachy was the obvious but reluctant choice of spokesman. He was a sick man, but as the friend of Bernard could plead as no other, Ireland's cause with the Cistercian Pope Eugenius III. There were, though, political difficulties, and royal emnity would not allow him to pass through England where the Augustinian canons at Guisborough were friends of old standing. King Stephen, it appeared, had fallen out with Eugenius III over an appointment to York, and interference with Malachy's Roman visit would be on a par with his admittedly senescent spite in attempting to prevent Theobald of Canterbury from attending a synod at Reims only a few weeks before. The ailing Malachy, then, had to take ship from Scotland to the Low Countries and it was a dying man who presented himself at Clairvaux to die a fortnight later in the arms of Bernard himself (1/2 November 1148). The blow to the cause of the reform was a heavy one, and the more so because Malachy was still relatively young.

In 1149 Murtagh Mac Loughlin hosted to Dublin where the Ostmen appear to have been embroiled in dynastic dissension, and his overlordship was recognised not only by the Dubliners but also by their nominal suzerain Dermot Mac Murrough. The following year saw the O Neill king encamped near Slane accompanied thither by Tighernan O Rourke and Donagh O Carroll as well as by the princes of Ulster proper. From the Boyne he proposed striking westwards into Connacht, but Turlough O Connor realised that he had not the resources to oppose Mac Loughlin with any prospect of success, and gave hostages. The O Neill king was thus recognised as overlord by four of the historic 'fifths', Munster alone holding aloof. Meath was once more partitioned, O Rourke and O Carroll receiving their reward while O Connor's acquiescence in the new order was bought by assigning him a share which it was hoped would give Connacht an enduring vested interest in maintaining the *status quo*. That Munster's turn was to come was obvious, and Turlough O Brien got in the first blow by invading Meath where resentment of partition was widespread. His Connacht namesake, however, was quick to support Mac Loughlin's settlement, and Munster was glad to obtain a year's truce through the mediation of the Dubliners. Once again there was family dissension within the O Briens, and Turlough only with difficulty retained his control of Thomond. In Desmond, too, a new threat to O Brien hegemony in Munster had appeared in the person of a Dermot Mac Carthy whose father and brother had died in captivity a decade before. O Brien once again took the offensive, and at first was everywhere successful. Dermot, however, invoked the assistance of Turlough O Connor and of Dermot Mac Murrough each in his own way menaced by the prospect of an O Brien-dominated Munster, and the combined armies of Connacht and Leinster invaded the province where O Brien had bottled up Mac Carthy at Cork. The O Brien army's one thought now was to get away and fight in Thomond where the people would not be hostile, but heavy mists lay in the gap between the Boggeragh and Nagles Mountains to the south of Mallow, and at Moin Mór, near Mourne Abbey, Turlough O Brien blundered into a trap set by his opponents. He himself escaped, but with only one in three of his followers. There was nothing that Thomond could do but sue for peace, and Turlough O Connor returned home in triumph accompanied by hostages from Munster and Leinster. He was master of three of the historic 'fifths', but any dreams he may have had of assuming once again the High Kingship were rudely shattered when Murtagh Mac Loughlin called a halt to the Connacht resurgence by invading what is now Sligo. An accommodation was arrived at whereby O Connor handed over to Mac Loughlin the Leinster hostages and added others of his own. For all practical purposes Murtagh Mac Loughlin was High King of Ireland.

In the meantime the work of reforming the Church continued, and in 1150 Eugenius III received a petition for the *pallia* on the same general lines as that which had been in the course of transmission when Malachy had died at Clairvaux on the road to Rome. The document seems to have been broadly based and generally representative of the state of affairs then obtaining in Ireland, and secular involvement and even endorsement may perhaps be inferred from what eventually resulted. An Italian, John Cardinal Paparo, was appointed papal legate, and in 1150 found his passage to Ireland barred by the English king. Again there is no reason to think that Stephen was particularly concerned for any ploys that he or his subjects may have had in Ireland; it was enough that the Cardinal represented the Pope who had thwarted the king's designs in the matter of the archdiocese of York. In 1151 Cardinal Paparo at last reached Ireland, by way of Northumberland and Cumberland then under Scottish control, having been received with every honour at the court of David I in

Carlisle. He consulted for a week with the saintly Gelasius of Armagh, and then moved south in the company of Christian O Conarchy, the Clairvaux-trained monk and former disciple of Malachy whose experience as first abbot of Mellifont and now as bishop of Lismore rendered him the ideal mentor for an Italian prelate anxious to master the Irish scene. A synod was convened which met first at Kells in Meath on 9 March 1152 but which adjourned a few days later to Mellifont. There are believed to have been present no fewer than 22 bishops and five bishops-elect, and an independent document from the continent gives what appears to be an authoritative listing of the 37 sees which were ratified or created on this occasion. The last included Kells itself, a church with particular associations with Columcille, and it cannot well be a coincidence that the old *paruchia* of the saint, a loose confederation of houses with Columban origins or connections, was in the process of a most edifying reform from within which was spear-headed by the Derry abbot Flaherty O Brollaghan. On his succession in 1150 he had made a circuit of the north to receive the customary Columban offerings – shades of Celsus as coarb of Patrick a generation before – and he seems to have obtained for his purely Irish foundations the exempt jurisdictions which were so critical in canon law for European monasticism and for the Cistercians and Cluniacs in particular.

The surprise package which Cardinal Paparo brought to Kells was Rome's recognition of four and not just two metropolitan sees. To Armagh and Cashel were to be added Tuam and Dublin, an arrangement that may be thought to mirror the Irish politics of 1150 rather than of 1152. Armagh was to have ten suffragan sees to use modern terminology, Ardagh, Clogher, Clonard, Connor, Down, Duleek, Kells, Kilmore ('Darnth'), Maghera and Raphoe. Duleek soon vanished, and the see of Maghera was later transferred to Derry, while the see of Clonard later took the name of Meath. Otherwise the only significant change down the centuries beyond the coalescence of Down and Connor would be the erection of the see of Dromore. The sees lost by Armagh to Tuam were Tuam itself, Clonfert, Cong and Killala, and here there was considerable reorganisation. Six suffragan sees were created or ratified, Achonry, Clonfert, Elphin ('Roscommon'), Killala, Kilmacduagh and Mayo. Mayo has since disappeared, swallowed up by Tuam along with an abortive Connemara see of Annaghdown which did not survive the Reformation, and Kilmacduagh has coalesced with the post-Penal see of Galway. Cashel was assigned twelve suffragans, Ardfert, Cloyne, Cork, Emly, Kilfenora, Killaloe, Limerick, Lismore, Roscrea, Ross, Scattery Island and Waterford, and in addition there was limited recognition of the claims of Ardmore, eventually allowed though the see, never viable, was soon swallowed up by Lismore, and of Mungret which was once more unlucky. There have been amalgamations down the centuries, with Kilfenora transferred to the province of Tuam and included with the see of Galway, and the see of Ardfert is known today as that of Kerry, but two-thirds of the names still figure in the titles of Irish bishops. Lost to Cashel were the Raith Bresail sees of Ferns, Glendaloch, Kildare, Kilkenny and Leighlin which were grouped together under Dublin but it would seem with very little change in their boundaries. Today Leighlin goes with Kildare, and Kilkenny passes under the title of Ossory, while Glendaloch was an early victim of the ambitions of the Norman metropolitans. Broadly, though, the pattern imposed on the Irish Church by Eugenius III is the pattern that has endured.

That Tuam received the pallium scarcely surprises. Turlough O Connor had been High King of Ireland albeit with opposition, and could well be so again. That Armagh's jurisdiction was limited at a time when Mac Loughlin looked like reviving an O Neill High Kingship is understandable. Malachy would seem to have had more difficulties on his own doorstep as it were than further afield, and the Pope cannot have regarded with equanimity the prospect of a Mac Loughlin High King allying himself with the remnants of Clann Sinaich to exercise political and spiritual dominion over half the island. If, too, the northern province was divided, justice and the look of the thing combined to indicate a division of Cashel's jurisdiction. Within Leinster Dublin could be thought of as holding the balance of power between two rival lines of kings, one in eclipse and the other represented by the reprobate Dermot Mac Murrough. Moreover, and this may have influenced Eugenius III as well as his advisers within the Irish hierarchy, the sending of the pallium to Dublin ended once and for all any dreams that Canterbury might still have entertained in respect of her old claim to ultimate jurisdiction over the Irish Church. It is noteworthy in this connection that at Kells the papal legate went out of his way to accord Armagh the primacy 'of the whole of Ireland'. Dublin was included in this definition, but it was a Dublin which knew very well that Canterbury would never have procured for an adopted daughter this symbol of papal approval of her metropolitan status.

The Synod of Kells, though, was not concerned just with the shaping of the Irish hierarchy, even if that impression is given by the non-survival of the official report of the proceedings. We have a few hints, however, as to the nature of the other business. Some Irish anomalies seem to have been criticised, for example the quite extraordinary precedence enjoyed by the abbesses of Kildare as coarbs of Brigid, and there were also predictable condemnations of simony and of clerical concubinage. The last must be seen in the context of continuing reluctance to make over to the new bishops the patrimonies of the old monastic Church, and when we find still being reported instances of married bishops we must infer in most cases the survival of coarbs rather than back-sliding among the new celibate occupants of sees identical in name with the old houses. For all this, the endowment of the Church continued to be a major problem, and it is significant that tithe as such should now be mentioned. Until the Irish church could be parished, its finance would always be precarious, and one of the as yet unanswered problems of twelfth-century Irish history is the extent to which the new bishops had been able to organise their new sees into deaneries and parishes before the arrival on the scene of the Anglo-Normans. The pattern probably varied from diocese to diocese, depending in part on the priority given to the task by the individual bishop, partly on his ability and energy, and partly on the degree of co-operation offered by the local secular power. That usury was denounced may mean only that the synod was attempting to conform to the contemporary European model, but certainly a problem in Ireland as nowhere else in Western Europe was public morality especially in relation to marriage. We must remember that elsewhere in Europe the Church was engaged in an uphill battle to rescue women from the more degrading consequences of the fuedalisation of society, and hence its particular concern with consanguinity, affinity and spiritual relationship. Even so, it is clear from a variety of sources that the marriage customs of Ireland were out of step with those of all her neighbours. There was, too a general lack of respect for public order, and the savage mutilation of rivals, often of the same kindred, to disqualify from kingly office was not likely to commend the Irish laity to clerics accustomed to the promotion of the so-called 'Truce of God' and 'Peace of God', and of other legislation designed to minimise the consequences of indiscriminate warfare and the introduction of more lethal weaponry.

For some reason Cardinal Paparo does not appear to have tarried in Ireland more than a few days after the closing sessions at Mellifont of the Synod of Kells, and by the end of March he was away to Scotland having first invested Christian of Lismore with his legatine status. The very same year saw the most celebrated perhaps of all the abductions of Irish history. Meath was as ever in ferment, and Murtagh Mac Loughlin marched south and was joined by his satellites Turlough O Connor and Dermot Mac Murrough. The kings of Ulster and Connacht fell out, Mac Murrough throwing in his lot with Mac Loughlin and O Connor receiving support from his traditional ally Tighernan O Rourke. The last was the scapegoat for the entire business, and for a time was dis-possessed from his lands. Rumour had it that between O Rourke's wife Dervorgilla, an O Melaghlin princess, and Dermot Mac Murrough there had been some youthful romance, but the lady was now in her middle forties, and one suspects that it was to hurt O Rourke and not to gratify lust that she was carried off to Leinster along with her dowry. Added piquancy is given to the incident by the circumstances that the abductor's wife was the sister of the abbot of Glendaloch and future reforming archbishop of Dublin, Laurence O Toole. Whatever transpired in Ferns, and Dervorgilla's age might have precluded the concep-tion of the ultimate in embarrassment, the union did not last long. To his credit Turlough O Connor intervened, and in 1153 Dervorgilla – and her fortune – was restored to Tighernan. There is much to commend the view that her brother had been privy to the whole affair; the O Melaghlins were a divided family with their backs to the wall, and a Leinster alliance could have rescued them from some at least of their difficulties. However this may be, Dervorgilla was taken back by her husband, and her good name seems not to have been compromised at least where the Church was concerned – by some accounts she had at least shouted for help when carried off. Not unnaturally, though, O Rourke was to be henceforth Mac Murrough's implacable enemy.

43

Murtagh Mac Loughlin was by now beyond doubt the most powerful force in Irish secular politics, and his new policy was to try and reconstruct Meath as a balance to Leinster and a buffer to Connacht. This was particularly desirable when Connacht and Leinster were king-making in Munster where Tadhg O Brien had once more rebelled against his brother Turlough, and the latter read aright the Ulster king's fears and invoked his assistance. The Mac Loughlin armies came south, Turlough was restored, and Tadhg blinded. O Connor's troops were defeated in the field, and so another blow struck at Connacht's prestige. The ageing Turlough O Connor, though, could not afford to stand by while Mac Loughlin built up Meath by transferring to it Leinster lands on the Munster mearing and so opening up a corridor from Thomond to and from the north, and in 1154 the Connacht fleet began to harry the Ulster coastline. Mac Loughlin's reply was to bring in a fleet from the Scottish Isles, but this was annihilated. The Connacht admiral, however, fell in the hour of victory, and Mac Loughlin hosted as far as Roscommon, traversed Breifne, and made a triumphal entry into Dublin. Ulster's hold on the northern half of the island was once again clear for all to see.

Outside Ireland at this juncture moves were afoot which in the long run were to be of the utmost consequence for an island where warfare had become endemic. In England the death of Stephen meant that Ireland's most powerful neighbour passed finally into the orbit of the Angevin Empire, and Henry's II's personal position was unchallenged and unchallengeable. At Rome Eugenius III had been succeeded by Adrian IV, an Englishman with legatine experience in Scandinavia but also a 'black monk' who would not be expected to be particularly well-disposed towards the Cistercian-dominated reform of the Irish Church. The combination of developments was not necessarily sinister, but there was a Bec tradition at

Canterbury that had always inclined to theories of wider jurisdiction even if Theobald himself had most probably forgotten the bishop Patrick incident of more than a decade before. For a time, though, English king and English Pope played almost childishly with theoretical dominions which in other circumstances might have evaporated without leaving a permanent scar on Anglo-Irish relations. It is possible that Ireland figured in Henry's calculations as a possible area of operations for a younger brother William who was as yet without an appropriate inheritance, but more probable that simple geographical tidiness dictated a concept of an Angevin Empire which would stretch from Atlantic to Mediterranean. On the Pope's side there would have been a genuine enough concern for the Irish Church and also for Christendom. It was not edifying that there should be professing loyalty to the Holy See an island where report had it that bishops were married, church-lands in lay occupation, clerics open to physical assault – the primate himself bore the marks of an attack on his person by the pious king of Oriel – and the marriage laws of the Church openly disregarded. In 1155 Adrian IV delivered himself of the momentous document known as the bull *Laudabiliter*. In it the state of the Irish Church was repeatedly denounced, papal overlordship of Ireland claimed in virtue of the Donation of Constantine, and Henry II authorised to enter on his own – had John of Salisbury, Theobald's secretary and one of Henry's emissaries, played the Arthurian card? – in order that the Church might be cleansed of abuse. An emerald ring accompanied the letter, and there can be little doubt that Henry II was given the free hand sought if and when he should decide on an invasion of Ireland. Fortunately for Ireland, when the business was discussed at Winchester around Michaelmas, Henry's mother was still alive, the redoubtable Matilda, daughter of Henry I, grand-daughter of William the Conqueror, widow of a German Emperor, and a former 'Lady of the English'. Not for her, nor for a son of her's, a cardboard kingdom lying outside the orbit of the civilised world and of her own experience, and her hard-headed opposition to the scheme brought her son's council back to reality. The project was shelved, and the copy of *Laudabiliter* filed away in the royal archives without any expectation that it would ever again see the light of day. There were real and urgent affairs of state in England and in France to claim the young king's attention, and for Ireland the moment of danger had passed even though it is doubtful if there were any in Ireland conscious of what had been afoot at the English court and Roman curia equally remote from the Irish way of life.

In Ireland things seemed to change not at all. Turlough O Connor continued the attempt to control Munster, and early in 1156 a Connacht fleet mustered on Lough Derg procured a grudging recognition of his overlordship by the Turlough O Brien he was no longer strong enough to depose. A new understanding was arrived at with O Rourke who could not but regard with fear as well as disfavour the continuing *entente* between Murtagh Mac Loughlin and Dermot Mac Murrough. On 20 May 1156, however, the old O Connor king breathed his last, and significantly it was to Clonmacnois and not to the new cathedral at Tuam that he was borne for burial. He was a man of the old order of things and even something of an anachronism. The association of his name with the Cross of Cong and so with a relic of the True Cross is a link with Constantine the Great, and like Constantine he had known what it was to put to death a son. It was another son, Rory, who had been more fortunate when detected in conspiracy who now succeeded him. The destinies of Ireland lay in consequence with four men singularly unmatched in ability and integrity, the young Rory, Murtagh Mac Loughlin, Tighernan O Rourke and Dermot Mac Murrough. Only one, the newcomer to the scene, would die a Christian death in his own bed, and he was to outlive the others by nearly two decades. What was common to all four men was a streak of ruthless cruelty. Even Rory's own succession was the occasion of a brother's blinding.

It was against this umpromising background that the reform of the Church continued. In 1157 the new abbey-church at Mellifont was solemnly consecrated. Christian was there as papal legate, Gelasius as primate, and the metropolitans of Dublin and Tuam. Mac Loughlin came as High King, Donagh O Carroll as founder and chief patron. The most distinguished benefactress was Dervorgilla who brought her husband with her. In 1158 Mac Loughlin himself chaired a synod held at Bri mic Taidg near Trim which ratified Flaherty O Brollaghan's labours to reform the *paruchia* of Columcille, an O Neill saint, so that too much should not be read into this layman's presidency. In 1154 a fire had destroyed the Augustinian house at Ferns which only very recently had been founded by Dermot Mac Murrough. It is suggestive of the influence of the reform that Dermot was not discouraged, and in 1160 or thereabouts the house was rebuilt and received a munificent endowment. The terms of the grant have survived, and the document reads like a contemporary charter from England or the Continent. The signatories range across church and state, but perhaps the most interesting is not the papal legate but an individual Latinising his name 'Florentius' and styling himself the king's chancellor. Admittedly Leinster was the most susceptible of the Irish 'fifths' to influences from overseas, but a decade before the Anglo-Norman invasion we can here see Irish secular society making some attempts itself to come to terms with the outside world. That its institutions were not all that different in character if not in their evolution may be inferred from the fact that standard feudal terminology does not flow too awkwardly from the chancery clerk's pen. Mac Murrough, though, was not just a vulgar seeker of the novel and foreign at the expense of tradition. Under his auspices there was compiled the greater part of the great anthology of literature and history more correctly styled *Lebor na Nuacongbála* ('The Book of Noughaval') which is still perhaps better known as the *Book of Leinster*. Particularly associated with its composition were Aedh O Crohan of Terryglass and the Cistercian bishop of Kildare, Finn O Gorman. Mac Murrough's crimes had by no means forfeited him the good-will of the Church to which he could show himself a generous if not entirely disinterested patron.

By 1159 Rory O Connor had consolidated his hold on Connacht, and was beginning to have ambitions in respect of territories to the east of the Shannon. His natural ally was O Rourke increasingly menaced by the power of Mac Loughlin who in turn was allied with Tighernan's old enemy, Dermot Mac Murrough. A battle at Ardee, however, went decisively in favour of Ulster, and Connacht losses were heavy. A subsequent meeting of the Connacht and Ulster kings near Ballyshannon did not resolve their difficulties. In the south-west, on the other hand, Turlough O Brien felt free to resume old aspirations to a kingdom of Munster, and in 1161 the Thomond army invaded Desmond where the Mac Carthy power was only a shadow of its former glory. That Connacht did not support Desmond at this juncture was perhaps due to Rory's preoccupation with the lands on the left bank of the Shannon – the Athlone 'bridgehead' critical for the '*Drang nach Osten*' which alone could drive a wedge between Mac Loughlin in Ulster and Mac Murrough in Leinster. To secure it, Rory was prepared to concede the shadow to obtain the substance, and he made a formal submission to Murtagh in return for Mac Loughlin recognition of his footing in Westmeath. Time was to vindicate this policy. Also in 1161 a minor synod was held at Derver hard by Kells in Meath which concerned itself with the position of the *paruchia* of Columcille as regards the hierarchies of Meath and Leinster. The houses in question received what would correspond today to exemption from normal diocesan jurisdiction, another victory for the reformers even though it must have suited the political ambitions of Mac Loughlin to see this endorsement of O Brollaghan's life-work. It was precisely in the Midlands that the protagonists in the next contest for the High Kingship were sparring to obtain strategic advantage.

The year 1162 saw continuing dissension within Desmond, but interest centres on the north of Leinster. Here Dermot Mac Murrough's most substantial achievement was the recognition of his sovereignty by the Ostmen of Dublin. It must have been a piquant occasion when we recall that the Dubliners had been responsible for his father's death. One account would even have it that in 1115 Donagh had been murdered by them in his own hall, but the more likely version is that he was killed in battle. Another diplomatic triumph for the Leinster king was the succession to the see of Dublin of his brother-in-law Laurence O Toole, abbot of Glendaloch. Mac Loughlin for his part evidently felt that Mac Murrough had a better chance of succeeding in thwarting O Connor designs on the Midlands, and it is possible that his own relations with the reformed Church of Armagh were again becoming strained. The same year there had come together at Clane on the Liffey a synod of the Irish Church at which there were present a total of 26 bishops. This reaffirmed the primacy of Armagh, made training in the school of Armagh obligatory for a certain class of lettered cleric on a national basis, and then solemnly condemned the descent of the coarbship of Patrick within the Clann Sinaich. The septuagenarian primate Gelasius was among the attendance, and one wonders whether he had reason to fear that Mac Loughlin contemplated on his death a revival of the old-style coarbship with a Clann Sinaich nominee. It is indeed curious that it was Mac Murrough and not Mac Loughlin who was the synod's lay protector, and that it should have discussed Ardmachian concerns so far from Armagh. In the following year interest reverts to Desmond with the final emergence of Dermot Mac Carthy as the strongest single contender for the monarchy following his murder of his first cousin, but an internecine war continued into 1164 when some sort of accommodation was only arrived at after yet another cousinly bloodbath. In Thomond, where Terryglass Abbey had been pillaged, there seems to have been discontent that advantage had not been taken of Desmond's difficulties, and in 1165 a palace revolution replaced Turlough O Brien by his son Murtagh, but the deposed king was able to escape to Desmond where he took refuge with Dermot Mac Carthy. Murtagh appealed for help to his overlord Rory O Connor and the Thomond and Connacht armies invaded Desmond. It is clear, though, that this massive intervention achieved very little, and one wonders in exactly what circumstances a Clare chieftain was killed and Shanagolden in Thomond burnt in the course of the same year. Murtagh Mac Loughlin, too, had his hands full, and it was only with difficulty that he suppressed a major rising in Ulidia. The leaders were spared thanks to the intercession of Donagh O Carroll whose position in Oriel was threatened by an O Neill power which was becoming more and more capricious. In 1166 the newly restored king of Ulidia, Eochaid Mac Dunleavy, fell again into Mac Loughlin's power and was blinded, and a number of his supporters massacred, in circumstances which constituted a flagrant violation of guarantees given by the Church of Armagh and by Oriel. Mac Loughlin's own people appear to have turned against him, and from Connacht and Breifne O Connor and O Rourke hosted across Meath to Dublin. Rory O Connor's High Kingship was accepted by the Ostmen with apparent enthusiasm, and having first turned north to

Mellifont to assure himself of Oriel's support, he took the Connacht host southwards to deal with Mac Murrough. The princes of North Leinster rallied to the support of the Connacht king, and Dermot conspicuously failed to hold a strong defensive position in the vicinity of Clonegall. The Connacht army, however, was cheated of a sack of Ferns when Dermot burnt the city to prevent it falling into O Connor hands, and Rory himself was anxious to return to the north in order to be master of the situation there. Dermot was not deposed, and four hostages satisfied the Connacht king who tarried only four days before marching to Donegal where he received the submission of the north-west. Mac Loughlin's position was now desperate. He was excommunicated and abandoned by many of his own, and the armies of Breifne and Oriel were virtually unopposed when they entered Ulster. Somewhere in the Fews he was hunted down and slain. In the hour of triumph the primate Gelasius showed a magnanimity worthy of the reform and all it had stood for, and the body of the High King received Christian burial at Armagh despite a colourful hunger-strike by Flaherty O Brollaghan and the community at Derry.

Less edifying was the implacability of O Rourke towards Mac Murrough. Rory O Connor's moderation was considered by Tighernan a betrayal, and in Meath, Dublin and North Leinster there were many who felt that justice had not been done. Connacht officially held aloof, an indication perhaps that O Connor was less in command of the situation than his title of High King might imply, and neither Ulster nor Munster was in any state to interfere. Dermot's friends melted away, and on 1 August 1166 the king and a few of his family and closest intimates took ship for England. This was indeed something of an innovation where the conventions of Irish feuding were concerned, and it is suggestive that the novel move should have been made in the part of Ireland which had always been in closest contact with the outside world. To contemporaries, however, it must have seemed the falling of the curtain rather than a prologue, and few outside Dermot's immediate circle would seem to have been other than relieved. Tighernan O Rourke had the satisfaction of slighting his old enemy's great palace-fortress at Ferns, an edifice of stone and perhaps even of ashlar, and South Leinster was partitioned between Dermot's brother Murrough and the king of Ossory, Donagh Mac Gilpatrick. The latter had also the custody of the older apparently of Dermot's legitimate sons, the luckless Enna, and all parties in the south-east appear to have sent hostages to Rory O Connor who was generally recognised as High King. The Connacht king's position must have seemed unassailable. The same year he made a solemn circuit round most of the island, and in 1167 he received the hostages of the Mac Loughlins after having presided at a great synod of the Irish Church held near Athboy in Meath. The archbishop of Cashel was the only absentee from among the metropolitans, and the lay attendance at Tlachtga, now the Hill of Ward, also included Dermot O Melaghlin of Meath, Tighernan O Rourke of Breifne, Magnus Mac Dunleavy of Ulidia, Donagh O Carroll of Oriel and Asgall Mac Torquil of Dublin. The concern of the synod was with the immunity of the Church and also with secular government, but the débâcle of the years that followed meant that such legislation was to be of purely academic interest. From Armagh Rory O Connor partitioned Ulster between two rivals, Niall Mac Loughlin and Aedh O Neill who received the western part of the province. In Munster, where in 1166 there had been a provincial synod at Lismore presided over by the papal legate Christian O Conarchy, the old rivalry between Thomond and Desmond was far from being extinguished. Murtagh O Brien was assassinated by one of his cousins in the Mac Carthy interest, and in 1168 O Connor imposed his own nominees on Thomond and Desmond alike, Donal O Brien, a brother of the murdered king who promptly blinded a third brother Brian, and the Dermot Mac Carthy who had dominated Munster politics for a number of years. The same year Rory set the seal on his High Kingship by presiding over a revived Fair of Tailtiu at Teltown between Navan and Kells. This was one of the oldest of Irish institutions, and the presidency had been for many centuries an O Neill prerogative associated with the Kingship of Tara. Since then the Fair had been usurped by Brian Bóromha in 1007 and by Turlough O Connor in 1120 or more probably 1121, auspicious precedents one might have thought, and certainly the sun had never shone more brightly on a son of Connacht. There was, however, one little cloud upon the horizon. In August 1167 Dermot Mac Murrough had slipped ashore at Glascarrig on the Wexford coast and with a few Anglo-Norman mercenaries made his way to Ferns. He had had little difficulty in regaining the territory held by his brother, and his old enemies had failed signally to move against him with appropriate dispatch. Dermot had thus been able to present Rory with a *fait accompli*, and a skirmish near Kellistown which went in favour of the High King's allies had not been sufficiently decisive to encourage them to undertake the weary task of reducing a sub-kingdom so clearly loyal to its natural lord. Dermot was tolerated in consequence as the petty king of ten cantreds only and on the condition that he forswore his claim to Leinster, recognised O Connor as High King, and last but not least paid O Rourke the very substantial sum of a hundred ounces of gold in compensation for the fifteen-year-old outrage against his marital honour.

3   Confrontation

A Muire as mor in gnim do ringned in hErind indiu . . .

THESE words open a short lament entered in the margin of
a page of the *Lebor na Nuacongbála* by a scribe, often
thought to be Aedh O Crohan himself, and deploring the
1166 expulsion of Dermot Mac Murrough. The very
ejaculation with which it begins epitomises the gap that
still existed between Ireland and the rest of Europe, for
there could be no better commentary on the failure of
feudalism to permeate the Irish way of life than the fact
that Irish still used 'Muire' where post-Feudal Europeans
would employ the titles 'Our Lady', 'Notre Dame',
'Unsehren Frauen', 'Nuestra Señora' or even 'Madonna'.
With the coming of the Anglo-Norman adventurers to
Ireland there was a confrontation of two societies, two
ideologies and two ways of life. In Ireland the theory at
least was that land was held inalienably by the family, and
that the various degrees of king bought support and sold
support with cattle to stock the land. The Irishman
instinctively reckoned his wealth in cattle, and a welcome
elasticity was given to an apparently inflexible framework
by the vagaries of murrain and rapine. With the breakdown
in public morality which had accompanied the repulse of
the Scandinavian onslaught there had been increasing
divergence between the theory and the reality, and it is
clear that large numbers of people could be and often were
dispossessed, and that something very like the concept of

'swordland' – possession by right of conquest – was prac-
tised if not expressed long before the twelfth century. The
Anglo-Norman, on the other hand, reckoned his wealth in
acres, and statutes of mortmain are a reminder of the
fossilisation of a system which at first sight seems flexible
enough. He held his land of a lord who might be the king
or himself a vassal at one or more removes from the king,
and he bought and sold his support by granting or being
granted land. Thus 'swordland' was something which he
well understood, and he was also prepared to concede a
measure of royal interference at all levels, this being in
marked contrast to Irish practice where in theory an over-
king, province-king and High King had no jurisdiction in
the internal concerns of their individual subject kingdoms.
Between the two systems there were, of course, many
points of resemblance – and we have seen that Dermot's
chancery had little difficulty in adapting feudal language to
Irish relationships – but these superficial likenesses themselves were to prove a fertile soil for the sowing by native
and newcomer alike of a whole crop of misunderstanding
and of misrepresentation.

When on or about 1 August 1166 Dermot Mac
Murrough took ship for foreign parts, it seems from the
first to have been with some idea of what needed to be
done. Nor was it an accident that he made his way to
Bristol. As we have seen, he had been a generous patron
of the Augustinian canons, and at Bristol there was in fact
an Augustinian house which could be counted upon to
offer at least temporary hospitality. Its founder and patron
was a prominent Bristol citizen Robert Fitz Harding, and
Fitz Harding had been a close friend of Henry II for nearly
a quarter of a century. Here was the necessary introduction,
but unfortunately Henry II was in France, and to find him
proved no easy matter as the restless Angevin moved hither
and thither around his French territories. In the early
spring of 1167 Dermot caught up with him in Aquitaine,

and Henry II graciously listened to his tale of woe. The Irish exile swore fealty, recognising the English king as his overlord, and sought English backing in return. Henry, however, was preoccupied with his continental ambitions, and could not spare the necessary men let alone come himself. He was, however, reluctant to shut the door on eventual intervention, and he may have recalled that a continual problem on the Welsh marches in particular had been underemployed knights impoverished by the Welsh resurgence under kings such as Rhys ap Gruffud but reluctant to undertake disciplined service in France. If Dermot could mop up a few of these motley heroes and remove them to Ireland, the door could be kept open and in the meantime the cause of good government of the Welsh marches made very much easier. Accordingly the Irish king was given money, authority to recruit, and his polite dismissal. Dermot returned to Bristol, but was disappointed with the local response to the royal permisssion to enlist. In the end, however, he was approached by Richard fitz Gilbert de Clare, earl of Striguil and erstwhile earl of Pembroke, who today is universally known as Strongbow though the nickname is properly his father's. Strongbow was sulking in part because the Pembroke title had been annulled as a Stephen creation even though his father had broken with that king, and in part because Henry had assigned to one of his cousins lands to which he thought he was entitled. In fact the lands had been largely overrun by the Welsh, and in any case Strongbow was not prepared to let too overt resentment prejudice his title to the not insignificant honour of Striguil around Chepstow. The two men conferred and eventually agreed that the Anglo-Norman would come to Ireland in the spring of 1168 and re-instate Dermot in Leinster. In return he would have the hand of Dermot's daughter Eva ('Aoife') and succeed to Leinster on Dermot's death. In Irish law such a succession would have been unthinkable, even if Dermot had not had two sons, Enna, a hostage in Ossory, and Conor, not to mention an illegitimate son Donal Cavanagh who was at this very moment looking after his father's interests back in Ireland. We may suppose that both sides agreed not to differ at this stage into how the succession could be manipulated, and Dermot's good faith must seem very doubtful. For his part Strongbow had his reservations. Dermot was waving on high his licence to recruit, but the Norman knew very well that he was a cut and more above the class of adventurers which his liege lord Henry had in mind, and unlike them he had something to lose. Probably still disappointed at the lack of response – Strongbow would first accompany Henry II's daughter on the first stage of her journey to marry a German duke – Dermot went into South Wales. Here he found the situation more favourable. Rhys ap Gruffud had on his hands a real problem in the person of Robert fitz Stephen, an Anglo-Norman adventurer with a Welsh mother who had been his prisoner for some three years but who was also his cousin. Fitz Stephen had been offered his freedom if he would serve against his lord the English king, but was having scruples. Dermot offered service in Ireland, and the alternative proved acceptable to ap Gruffud who wanted to be rid of this embarrassing kinsman. As it happens, South Wales was littered with fitz Stephen's mother's connection by a succession of husbands and lovers of whom Stephen was not even the last. As the mistress of Henry II Nesta had had two sons, Meiler and Robert, and by Gerald of Barry two sons and a daughter, Maurice, David and Angharat. Meiler, Robert and Maurice were all more or less at a loose end, and eventually were to find their way to Ireland. David was the bishop of St Davids but had a son Milo who would also be free to come, while Angharat sent two sons of whom the younger, Gerald of Barry, better known perhaps as Giraldus Cambrensis ('Gerald of Wales'), was to be the chronicler of the invasion. Maurice and David too, had been persuasive advocates for Robert's release for the Irish venture, and associated with them was a third half-brother, this time by another mother, William fitz Gerald whom Nesta appears to have reared as her own. He himself did not participate in the expedition, but sent a son Raymond le Gros, though as it happens in the distant future the descendants of others of his progeny would leave an even more enduring scar on Ireland. It is curious but significant that Nesta's children by a Welsh father seem not to have been drawn into Dermot's enterprise – it was the Norman blood and especially the Geraldine which seems to have been critical. The bargain struck with 'Nesta's brood' was similar to that concluded with Strongbow. Robert fitz Stephen and Maurice fitz Gerald of the older generation were to bring a force to Ireland in the spring of 1168 and support Dermot in his recovery of Leinster. In return they would receive the town of Wexford and two adjacent cantreds.

From South Wales Dermot was in contact with his supporters in Leinster, and reports from them in the summer of 1167 encouraged him to return, as we have seen, in advance of his new allies. A handful of the type of mercenary envisaged by the English king did accompany him, the leader being Richard fitz Godebert de Roche, a Fleming from the Anglo-Norman colony in Pembrokeshire and the ancestor of the Munster Roches. South Leinster rallied to him, but Rory O Connor's hosting precluded the wider ambitions he nurtured, and he could count himself fortunate to be allowed to retain a petty kingdom not much larger than the modern Co. Wexford. Vulnerable now as well as thwarted, Dermot sent his O Regan chancellor over to South Wales to urge early intervention by the Geraldines whom he rightly judged to be more enthusiastic for the Irish campaign than Strongbow. Honour, too, was a compelling motive where fitz Stephen was concerned, and early in 1169 the newly liberated knight began to assemble what troops he could. By the end of April he had some 90 horsemen and 300 men-at-arms and archers to serve on foot. On 1 May or thereabouts they disembarked from three ships at Bannow Bay. With them as a species of commissar to report on progress to Strongbow and to see that his interests were not prejudiced was an uncle, Hervey de Montmorency. The following day two ships brought Maurice de Prendergast with 10 horses and a considerable body of infantry and archers. Dermot was apprised of their arrival, and Donal Cavanagh arrived, soon to be followed by his father with 500 men, while an uncertain number were recruited from the immediate vicinity. Wexford was the first objective, and as they approached the Wexford Ostmen marched out to give battle only to recoil when the composition of the attacking force became clear. The suburbs were fired to deprive the besiegers of cover, and the line of the wall held against the first assault. The day's operations concluded with the wanton destruction of merchant shipping in the harbour, and the following day fitz Stephen was preparing to renew the assault when emissaries came out from the town to seek terms. Two bishops are supposed to have lent their services, and Wexford surrendered and gave four hostages. Fitz Stephen and fitz Gerald shared the town and its immediate hinterland, and Montmorency received two cantreds to the south-west. The victorious army then moved to Ferns, and three weeks later Dermot, his army swollen by contingents from South Leinster returning to his banner, proposed an attack on Ossory where Donal Mac Gilpatrick the previous year had blinded Dermot's unfortunate son Enna. The first campaign nearly ended disastrously in the forests between the Barrow and the Nore south of Kilkenny, but the position was restored by the coolness of Prendergast and 200 heads of Mac Gilpatrick's soldiers were brought to Dermot whose exultation knew no bounds. Returning first to Ferns, the South Leinster army next went up the Slaney and into Kildare and plundered the O Phelans and O Tooles before swinging east to Glendaloch and the sea. A second invasion of Ossory appears to have been up the Slaney, down the Burren, and thence to the valley of the Dinin and over the Nore to the vicinity of Freshford. Mac Gilpatrick was driven from his prepared positions after hard fighting, and once again Dermot returned to Ferns with huge booty. His Anglo-Norman allies, on the other hand, had less cause for satis-faction. Cattle-tributes were of little interest to them, and these land-avid men had no intention of becoming mere mercenaries fighting in purely Irish causes. Reports were coming in of a great hosting by Rory O Connor, and Prendergast indicated to Dermot that he and 200 of his men had had enough and wished to depart for Wales. Dermot instructed the Ostmen of Wexford to ensure that the necessary shipping would not be available, whereupon Prendergast offered his services to a delighted Mac Gilpatrick. Donal Cavanagh was sent off to oppose with 500 men any junction between Prendergast and Mac Gilpatrick, but the mainly Flemish contingent broke through the gap between the White Mountain and the Barrow and concluded an alliance with the Ossory sub-king at St Mullins. Rory's hosting swept into the plain of Wexford, and Dermot and fitz Stephen sought the protec-tion of the forests at the foothills of Mount Leinster. An attempt was made to seduce fitz Stephen from his allegi-ance, while another promised Dermot Leinster if only he would betray his Anglo-Norman allies. Both proposals were spurned, but ultimately a peace was concluded whereby Dermot recognised Rory as High King and surrendered his son Conor as hostage. In return he was to have freedom of action in Leinster – presumably in the hope that the now divided Anglo-Normans would decimate each other – and Dermot further agreed privately that he would divest himself of his foreign allies at the first opportunity. Then and only then was Conor to receive in marriage one of Rory's daughters. Left to hold his own corner, Mac Gilpatrick supported by Prendergast attacked the O Mores in Laois and promptly appealed to Dermot who marched north with fitz Stephen. Prendergast counselled withdrawal, and the men of Ossory began to complain of the expense of foreigners who would not withstand men of their own race. Mac Gilpatrick reported to Prendergast a plot to massacre the foreigners, and when they attempted to leave for home it was reported to them that an ambush had been set. Prendergast threw the ambushers off their guard by announcing that his troops had decided after all to continue in the Irish service, but taking horses the Flemings rode away for all they were worth and reached Waterford whence they took ship for Wales.

Dermot once again had a monopoly of Anglo-Norman mercenaries, and in 1170 decided to secure his position in North Leinster by bringing the Dubliners to heel. Fitz Stephen was left to hold Wexford, and fitz Gerald accompanied Dermot on a campaign which devastated the Dublin hinterland before the Ostmen returned to their obedience. In the meantime there had been developments in Munster which lay outside his sphere of influence, though Donal Mór O Brien in Thomond was his son-in-law. The ambitious and able Donal had chosen this moment to repudiate his O Connor allegiance in order to prosecute his designs on Desmond, and Rory mobilised a great fleet and prepared to crush so unlooked-for a challenge to his authority. In May there arrived at Baginbun Raymond le Gros with 10 knights and 70 archers, an advance party for Strongbow who obviously feared that if he did not come soon to Ireland the real spoils would have passed into other hands. The Geraldines already in Ireland, however, were not in evidence, presumably because they were still away at Limerick helping Donal Mór to withstand Rory

61

who achieved little more than the burning of the bridge at Killaloe. Montmorency came into Baginbun with three knights and a few more men-at-arms and archers, and the advance party dug itself in, pending the arrival of Strongbow and the main army. The Waterford Ostmen realised that the seizure of a point so far to the west of Wexford boded ill for them, and decided to wipe out the newcomers before they could be reinforced. With the support of the O Phelans of Decies and others of the local Irish the Ostmen moved against Baginbun where the garrison was outnumbered by thirty to one. A sally from the fort miscarried, but Raymond's personal gallantry and enterprise saved the day, and a stampede of cattle broke the opposing ranks. Several hundred of the attackers were killed, and after some debate seventy prisoners were massacred. Not until August did the promised reinforcements come, but then it was to be on a scale beyond all expectation. Strongbow had wrung from Henry II a jesting consent to the enterprise, and had slipped away quietly before the king could change his mind. Even Prendergast was persuaded to stake another throw, and the total of the army recruited was of the order of 200 cavalry and 1,000 infantry and archers. Waterford was the objective, and on 23 August Strongbow disembarked his forces in the neighbourhood of Passage. He was joined by Raymond and some of the tiny garrison at Baginbun, and on 25 August the siege of Waterford began and ended. A weak point in the defences was soon exploited, and through the gap the Anglo-Normans poured with bitter hand-to-hand combat ending in the capture of the city and the summary execution of two of the most prominent of the citizens. Other notable prisoners were only spared at the intercession of Dermot who was at once informed of the city's capture and arrived on the scene accompanied by fitz Stephen and Maurice fitz Gerald. A council of war decided that the next objective should be Dublin. First of all, however, there were existing engagements to be honoured, and in the cathedral of Waterford Strongbow and Eva were duly married.

Strongbow's position in the autumn of 1170 was uncomfortably delicate. Even as his army was leaving Milford Haven, messengers had arrived from Henry II bidding him desist from the enterprise, and the forfeiture of the lordship of Striguil was a very real possibility. On paper he might be Dermot's heir, and the kingship of Leinster, again on paper, was a prize worth many earldoms, but it was in Ireland an unheard of thing for an inheritance to pass in the female line. Where his future subjects were concerned even the bastard Donal Cavanagh's title would be superior, and, the blinded Enna apart, there was the legitimate Conor, admittedly a hostage at the court of the High King, not to mention a loyal if prudently self-effacing brother Murrough. At this juncture Dublin could well prove the key to the whole situation. The Ostmen of that city had the one major fleet in the Irish Sea. Under Dermot's control it could dispute the passage of any expedition that Henry II might send against his mutinous feudatories. Under other leadership it could cut the Anglo-Norman lines of communication with Wales and England, and bring succour to the Ostmen of Wexford and Waterford resentful of their new masters. Word reached the Dubliners of Strongbow's intentions, and they invoked the High King's assistance. Rory had been baulked of his prey in Munster by fitz Stephen's intervention, but an uneasy stalemate between Thomond and Desmond meant that he could safely mobilise a formidable host against the Anglo-Norman advance into North Leinster. Supported by the men of Breifne, Meath and Oriel, the Connacht army took up a position at Clondalkin from which point it was hoped it would be possible for it to intercept Dermot should he come across on either side of the Dublin mountains. The allies, however, slipped through an unguarded pass and were under the walls of Dublin before Rory could adjust his dispositions. The ostmen considered themselves betrayed and sought terms, while for his part Rory considered the negotiations a repudiation of his High Kingship which absolved him from fighting on ground not of his choice. The result was that the Connacht army and the Midland contingents went home, and it was left to the unfortunate archbishop Laurence O Toole to get what terms he could for his flock from his redoubtable brother-in-law and the still more formidable Norman husband of his niece. For three days the negotiations continued before one contingent of the besiegers in flagrant violation of the truce rushed the defences on 21 September. They broke into the city which was given up to killing and pillage, though many of the inhabitants, including Asgall Mac Torquil, took to their ships and sailed away to Man and the Scottish Isles. It is not impossible that the vessels had already been laden with valuables and got ready for sea against precisely this sort of eventuality.

Dermot now turned his attention to Meath. At Easter Conor Mac Loughlin had been assassinated in the cathedral precincts at Armagh, and intervention from the north was unlikely pending clarification of the succession. The cause of a dispossessed Brega kinglet Donal O Melaghlin gave him an excuse to intervene, and the Leinster armies pillaged East Meath, including Clonard and Kells, before invading Breifne itself. Tighernan O Rourke, however, countered the move by executing the Meath hostages, and by the threat of abandoning O Connor to Dermot's tender mercies he compelled the High King to put to death the Leinster hostages who included Dermot's younger legitimate son Conor and a son of Donal Cavanagh. The Leinster army fell back on Dublin which was garrisoned by a small force of Anglo-Normans under Milo de Cogan, and Strongbow then proceeded to a Waterford increasingly menaced by the resurgent power of the Mac Carthys in Desmond. A fairly representative synod of the Church convened at Armagh by the saintly Gelasius could do little but deplore foreign intervention and suggest that it was God's punishment for past slave-raidings. Dermot back in Ferns mourned Conor's death, and a profound gloom must have settled on the Anglo-Normans of Leinster when tidings came of the English king's reactions to a campaign which had been as sensational as essentially indecisive. The adventurers were simply given until Easter 1171 to return to their homes, and an embargo was put on all sailings to Ireland. The penalty for defiance was to be forfeiture of their lands in England and France. The leaders, of course, had most to lose, and after consulting his colleagues Strongbow dispatched Raymond le Gros to Henry II in Aquitaine with a letter to remind the king that he had originally approved enlistment in Dermot's cause, and that Dermot had in fact done homage to Henry for Leinster. The writer went on to offer that he should hold his Irish lands directly of the English Crown as a pledge of his loyalty. Rightly Strongbow had diagnosed Henry's fear of too great subjects, and even more of tenants-in-chief passing out of his jurisdiction, and so escaping liability for service in the wars on the continent that were ever the Angevin preoccupation. Until, too, Henry II should reply, Strongbow and his adherents could argue that they were under no obligation to do anything concrete about the order of recall.

Raymond le Gros did not return to Ireland until the early summer 1171, and his report of Henry's continued insistence on the immediate return of the adventurers by then must have seemed magnificently irrelevant to changed circumstances. Dermot Mac Murrough had died at Ferns, by one account intestate, unshriven and impenitent, and Strongbow's premature succession was repudiated by all the Irish of Leinster. The only quislings were Donal Cavanagh, a dispossessed prince from Breifne, and a petty chieftain from Carlow. The High

King Rory more than countenanced this rejection of Anglo-Norman pretensions by hosting to Dublin, where a premature attack in May by the exiled Asgall Mac Torquil with the support of Vikings from the Scottish Isles had culminated in Asgall's execution in his own hall, and on this occasion he was supported by Domnall Mór O Brien from Munster and Magnus Mac Dunleavy from Ulidia. Possibly at Laurence O Toole's invitation, too, a squadron from Man blockaded the Liffey mouth, and for nearly two months Dublin was completely beleaguered. In the late summer Donal Cavanagh slipped through the pickets to bring news that Wexford had risen against fitz Stephen. Strongbow called his captains together, and it was agreed that he should offer to hold Leinster as Rory's man, but the High King was aware that provisions were running out and now insisted that Strongbow should be content with just the three Ostman settlements of Dublin, Waterford and Wexford. Many of the Irish troops were away on detached service, and the Anglo-Normans decided to risk all on one desperate throw, and 600 men slipped out unobserved along the Finglas road, wheeled and fell on Rory's camp at Castle-knock. The surprise was as complete as the ensuing rout, and the siege of Dublin broke up in confusion. Milo de Cogan was again left in command of the garrison, and Strongbow marched south to Wexford where fitz Stephen had been bottled up in a promontory fort at Carrick-on-Slaney. He had with him five men-at-arms and their supporting archers, and after a false report that Rory had taken Dublin he agreed to surrender on condition he received a safe-conduct overseas. Strongbow cut his way through an ambush near Mount Leinster and arrived to find Carrick fallen and the prisoners incarcerated on Beggerin Island. Wexford itself was in flames, and the Anglo-Norman relief force was informed that any further advance would result in the summary execution of fitz Stephen and the other prisoners. With heavy hearts Strongbow and his followers went on to Waterford and there planned a new series of attacks designed to bring Leinster into obedience. Time was running out as at any time Montmorency might return from a second mission to Henry II with bad tidings. In fact Strongbow's emissary had met the king at Argentan in July and achieved a measure of success. It was provisionally agreed that Strongbow should hand over to the Crown Dublin and Waterford and any other strongholds the king might name, but in return for this he was to be allowed to hold whatever else his marriage to Eva had brought him, and in addition he would receive back his confiscated lands on the Welsh march and in Normandy.

A campaign against Ossory with Donal Mór's support is chiefly memorable for a disgraceful attempt judicially to murder Mac Gilpatrick which was thwarted only by the courageous probity of Prendergast, and accommodations were arrived at both with Murrough Mac Murrough and Donal Cavanagh. In September Montmorency returned with Henry II's terms, and also the news that the king himself, at loggerheads with Rome over the murder of Becket, was on his way. Strongbow was advised to slip over to England and make his peace before Henry should see for himself the state of Ireland. The royal muster was at Newent in Gloucestershire and either there or at Pembroke king and earl met. To placate Henry, Strongbow had to add to what had already been conceded, Wexford, the Dublin hinterland and the Wicklow littoral as far as Arklow, and it was a warning to the Geraldines that Henry went out of his way to be gracious to Rhys ap Gruffud as he passed through South Wales. Michaelmas saw Henry at St Davids but the same night he was back at Pembroke though adverse winds delayed his sailing from Milford Haven until 16 October. He was accompanied by 500 horse and seven times that number of men-at-arms and archers. It was a full feudal hosting, and royal tenants who commuted actual service by scutage paid for the expedition to be equipped on a lavish scale. A siege-train was included which suggests that Henry still feared defiance from his Anglo-Normans who had or might soon have garrisons in all the walled towns of the Ostmen not excluding Limerick and Cork. By 18 October Henry was in Waterford and receiving Strongbow's formal homage. Leinster, the excepted territories apart, was henceforth the earl's on condition only that he sent a hundred knights when the king should ask for them. It was clear that a new star had risen in the Irish firmament, and political realists could not but contrast Henry's highly professional fighting-machine with the *ad hoc* levies of a High King's hosting. Rory O Connor just could not compete, and a few days later Dermot Mac Carthy presented himself at Waterford, swore fealty, offered hostages and tribute, and in return was guaranteed Desmond against all comers, land-hungry Anglo-Normans not excepted. As already promised before the king left England, the Wexford Ostmen handed over fitz Stephen who was soundly berated and almost ritually consigned to Reginald's Tower to await the king's pleasure, and Henry advanced to Lismore for a meeting with the papal legate to Ireland, Christian O Conarchy; a meeting the more piquant when we consider that one of Henry's last acts before leaving England had been to instruct his officers to refuse entry to papal legates investigating Becket's murder. The king then proceeded to Cashel where arrangements were concluded with the archbishop Donatus ('Donal') O Houlihan for the holding of a synod of the Irish Church in circumstances which it was hoped would convince the Pope that the English king, for all the unfortunate affair of Becket, was a zealous son of Rome. To Henry at Cashel there came, apparently again of their own volition, Donal Mór O Brien and the chief rival in Desmond to Mac Carthy, Donagh O Mahony. They did homage on much the same terms, and on paper at least Henry II was now overlord of Munster as well as Leinster.

While still at Lismore Henry had indicated to his Anglo-Normans that he considered them subject to the same laws as the English in England, and as he returned to Waterford and progressed northwards by easy marches to Dublin the ambiguous pattern of Irish submissions continued. The English king thought he was granting away his own property while the Irish princes believed they were merely obtaining for their family freeholds an effective royal guarantee against dispossession. Dublin was reached on 11 November, and Henry was able to keep Christmas in state in a palace run up outside the walls by Irish craftsmen. To Irish and Ostmen he was uniformly gracious, and submissions poured in from North Leinster, Meath, Louth and even Breifne and Ulidia. Meanwhile Christian was presiding over the synod at Cashel where the wide attendance included the archbishops of Cashel, Dublin and Tuam—Gelasius was by now too frail to travel from Armagh though he was to endorse the transactions. The emphasis of the synod was on public morality rather than Church organisation. A diocesan Church already parished was perhaps rather hopefully assumed to be the rule. The synod legislated on such matters as tithes, bequests, masses for the dead and baptisms which were very relevant to a parochially organised clergy, as well as on the old issues of the conflict of Christian morality and Irish tradition which centred on marriage law and the immunity of all clerics from tribute of any description and in particular from coshering. To this end the cleric was now formally released from his obligations as a member of a kindred to contribute to communal or collective fines. Open to misunderstanding was one major innovation. To secure liturgical uniformity it was essential to adopt a norm, and there was to hand a convenient model in the Sarum Use which the Irish bishops accepted not because it was English but because it was available and in accord with progressive thinking. There is no evidence that they were shown a copy of *Laudabiliter*, but each of the bishops did send under his own seal a recognition of Henry's ultimate overlordship of Ireland. The king was obviously and to some extent genuinely solicitous for the welfare of the Irish Church, and the bishops had a financial as well as spiritual interest in reform. By September Henry was to be reconciled with the Pope over the Becket affair, and from Tusculum in that month there came three papal letters. One congratulated the Irish hierarchy, another Henry himself, while the third praised the Irish princes who had accepted Henry as king. There was still pained concern, though, for Irish want of morality, and Alexander III was careful to observe that his strictures were based on the testimony of the bishops themselves.

Papal approbation, however, was something still very much in the future when Henry II had to leave Ireland for England where his presence was urgently required. A formidable conspiracy was simmering around his undutiful son, and the papal legates kicking their heels on the Continent were threatening to put England and Normandy under interdict. A stormy winter had virtually cut off Ireland from England, and when the news broke matters had obviously become very grave. Before sailing from Wexford on 17 April 1172, however, Henry had been able so to organise affairs in Ireland that he was reasonably confident that Strongbow's power was tamed. Hugh de Lacy, a newcomer to the scene, had been named the king's justiciar or viceroy, assigned the custody of Dublin, and, to give teeth to his authority, granted Meath on the same terms as Strongbow held Leinster except that the knight-service was halved. Four of 'Nesta's brood' were attached to the Dublin garrison, and it would be de Lacy's task to dispense from the rich lands of Meath a patronage with which the Leinster earl could not hope to compete. Dismemberment and dispossession would be nothing new to the O Melaghlins, and de Lacy could be relied on to get his own way even though in the end the invaders could only extinguish opposition by stringing up a certain Magnus, one of the abler and more persistent of competitors within the family for the title and the lands. Henry's obvious hope was that de Lacy's power and influence would grow at a greater rate than Strongbow's, and it is interesting to see his different attitudes towards Dublin and Waterford. The Ostmen of the latter city basked in the royal favour, doubtless to Strongbow's mortification, but at the future Irish capital the Ostmen were expelled from within the walls to Oxmantown and an English colony planted as an act of deliberate policy. Silent throughout remained Rory O Connor, the natural protector one would have thought of the Irish, and it is scarcely unjust to describe his attitude to events as that of a dozing man who believes a deluge to be no more than a bad dream. It was a year of murrain into the bargain, and the north was still recovering from events in the previous year when the adulterous Magnus Mac Dunleavy from Ulidia had invaded Mac Loughlin territory around Coleraine but been repelled and wounded, a preliminary to his assassination by his own brother. Together Connacht and Ulster might have been able to break the remorselessly tightening but – still over large areas – quite precarious Anglo-Norman grip on the remaining three of the 'fifths', but in fact Ireland was slipping through Rory's numbed and nerveless hands. By the end of 1172 Tighernan O Rourke had been removed from the scene by de Lacy treachery at the Hill of Ward near Athboy, his mutilated head and body being put on display at Dublin. Other victims of the now quite unscrupulous invaders were Donal O Farrell in what is now Co. Longford and Murrough Mac Murrough in Leinster. Henry II may not himself have connived at these acts, but if he had been able to devote more time and thought to Ireland he might have foreseen them as inevitable from the moment his officers were given a free hand to enfeoff Meath and Leinster. Equally blame-worthy were the Irish still to come into direct contact with the Norman power, and the Irish annals make sorry reading when they record the luxury of internal war within Ulster with the Mac Loughlins being heavily defeated when invading Donegal. It is a tribute, though, to Rory O Connor's personal rule in Connacht itself that the aged Gelasius was able to make a Patrician coarb's circuit there, and return safely to Armagh with the proceeds. More practically, perhaps, the just as saintly Laurence O Toole in Dublin was prepared to raise his voice in protest against the lawlessness of the Anglo-Norman lords, and it could well have been as a result of his representations that Henry II summoned both de Lacy and Strongbow in the spring of 1173 to serve with the feudal host in Normandy.

De Lacy's temporary replacement as justiciar was William fitz Audelm, a member of the royal household and a man very conscious of royal prerogatives. He it was who had published at a synod held at Waterford the three letters which had come from Alexander III. Giraldus gives the gist of a privilege allegedly uttered on the same occasion which could mean that a copy of *Laudabiliter* had been turned up in the files of the English royal chancery and been given an airing with the explanation that the new Pope was of the same mind as his predecessor. Little, though, is known of fitz Audelm's essentially caretaker administration, and in the autumn Strongbow returned to Ireland and took over the justiciarship which had been de Lacy's. The earl had somehow won Henry's favour, and it was almost as if the king wished to atone for his past hostility to the man who had after all master-minded the English invasion of Ireland. Not only was Strongbow permitted to bring back as his lieutenant Raymond le Gros whom the year before Henry had thought it prudent to remove from the Irish scene, but the useful ports of Wicklow and Wexford were restored to him. It is probably significant that Strongbow hence-forth left the hinterland of Dublin severely alone, re-cognising that area to be one excessively sensitive where the English king was concerned, and after a brief campaign in Kildare the earl turned his attentions to the south-west of his great lordship. In quite cynical violation of the submissions made to Henry not two years before Strong-bow's forces raided into the Decies, and a squadron from Cork was annihilated when it attempted to intercept a flotilla returning to Waterford with the spoils of Lismore. On shore Raymond le Gros inflicted a sharp defeat on Dermot Mac Carthy who had come to the support of his tributaries, and one is left feeling that Strongbow had been given licence by the king to do anything he liked provided only he kept away from Dublin and Meath where de Lacy's henchmen were securing potentially some of the best ploughland in Europe. In Thomond, though, Donal Mór O Brien exhibited exceptionally realistic farsightedness when he appreciated that any external attack on Desmond was an attack on Munster. Supported by a Connacht contingent under Conor O Connor, the High King's son, he struck down the valley of the Nore. At Kilkenny Strongbow had some sort of rudimentary fort hardly worth the name of castle, but the garrison thought discretion the better part of valour and evacuated the position without a fight. The Munster-men slighted the works and then withdrew. Smarting under the humiliation Strongbow now found himself deprived of the services of Raymond le Gros who commanded the confidence of his knights as no other of his lieutenants. Raymond had been refused the constableship of Leinster and the hand of the earl's sister, Basilia, and had come to the conclusion that his services were not sufficiently appreciated. Accordingly he took ship for Wales, his father's death affording a colourable pretext for his desertion at this crisis.

On 27 March 1174 Gelasius died at Armagh at the age of eighty-six, but the Anglo-Normans were in no position as yet to manipulate the succession. Nor apparently was the Irish hierarchy which could so advantageously have filled the vacancy by translation. The successor was an apparently well-connected local nonentity, Concors ('Conor') O Connolly, but his visit to Rome in the following year could suggest an incipient statesman seeking papal pressure on Henry II to bridle his Anglo-Normans. Unfortunately Concors like so many others from north of the Alps succumbed to the Italian climate, and his successor Gilla-in-Coimdhed O Carron was apparently another representative of purely local interests. In Munster the summer of 1174 witnessed a notable check to the Anglo-Norman advance. The Leinster army, captained now by the personally unpopular Montmorency, advanced into Tipperary and came to Cashel. Donal Mór O Brien, however, was still loyally supported by the High King, whose son Conor was again in the field in his support. Strongbow prudently waited for reinforcements to come up from Dublin, but Donal Mór and Conor fell on them near Thurles and slew as many as seven hundred. The Ostmen fighting on foot bore the brunt of the casualties, and we are not to imagine that the Irish had found the answer to the cavalry-charge supported by archers. Even so, Strongbow was unable to steady his troops, and the Leinster army fell back on Waterford. The Ostmen there, however, would seem to have been infuriated by reports that their Dublin cousins had been left to suffer such disproportionate losses, and the earl thought it prudent to remain outside the walls and to offer Raymond le Gros his sister's hand and the constableship if only he would return from Wales and take command. Raymond threw together a scratch force of several hundred cavalry and archers and sailed for Wexford where similar resentment of the Anglo-Normans was fast coming to a head. Strongbow and his army were then brought round to Wexford, while at Waterford there was a massacre of the Englishry of the place before the military garrison was able to restore order.

Shaken out of his usual inaction by the success at Thurles, the High King now prepared to host into Meath where O Melaghlin resentment of Anglo-Norman expropriation would guarantee a measure of local support. The new lords were in no position as yet to organise effective resistance, and de Lacy's tenantry streamed back towards Dublin before the Irish advance. There were as yet few major fortifications, and at Trim the *caput* or chief place of the Meath earldom, Hugh Tyrrell, de Lacy's castellan, decided that the unfinished works were in no shape to hold out any prospect of a successful defence, and they were abandoned. The O Connor host slighted the motte and burnt the hall, but on the approach of Strongbow with the army of Leinster the Irish withdrew, though not before a tactical defeat had been inflicted on their rearguard. Still the Anglo-Norman knights were masters of any field where they could group for a charge, and the combination of mailed men-at-arms and archers was in itself superior in normal circumstances to the indisciplined onrush of the Irish levies who relied on the dart and the axe. An uneasy truce followed with the protagonists counting the cost of a summer which had brought neither side any decisive advantage, and it was probably soon afterwards that there began talks between all the interested parties to see if some *modus vivendi* could be arrived at which would meet the situation. The High King was interested primarily in establishing his authority over his nearest neighbours, and old Connacht fears of Thomond beyond doubt loomed far too large on an unduly limited horizon. Strongbow and the absent de Lacy wanted time to develop their new earldoms, and particularly to build the network of minor castles which could hold up any Irish advance until help came, and at all times hold down such of the indigenous population as economic considerations made it desirable should remain. Henry II was still interested in playing off one earl against the other, but would not be sorry to see the old High King powerful enough to be a useful ally if his Anglo-Normans became too obstreperous. In the background fluttered the more enlightened of the reforming churchmen. The invasion and its aftermath were disrupting their attempts to consolidate their new dioceses, and it weighed with them that the policy of the English crown was to be just if not generous. Outstanding among them was Laurence O Toole of Dublin who combined breadth of outlook with a sincere devotion to his flock's best interests, and who never spared himself in his efforts to salvage something out of the wreckage for the Church which, if it could avoid crossing swords with the king, might well be the best bulwark of the people against the extortions of the newcomers.

The year 1175, then, saw Rory O Connor careful to do nothing that would prejudice the negotiations with Henry, while the leaders in Westmeath were quite cynically abandoned to the tender mercies of de Lacy's officers who carried out a whole series of punitive raids into those areas which they were not yet ready to colonise. As an outline settlement began to appear, Strongbow was brought over to England for consultations, and it was in his absence that the provisions of the peace were anticipated, in spirit at least, when the High King sought and obtained Anglo-Norman intervention in the affairs of Munster. Donal Mór O Brien of Thomond was becoming too powerful, and civil war among the Mac Carthys offered him a prospect of reasserting O Brien authority over Munster as a whole. He hosted as far as Killarney, and at about the same time secured his position within his kindred by blinding some distant cousins. In Ulster there was an invasion of Donegal by the O Neill tributaries to the east, and this meant that Rory O Connor had no worry for his left flank or rear. The Connacht army swept into Thomond, and from Ossory a small but choice division of Anglo-Normans and Irish under Raymond le Gros and Donal Mac Gilpatrick arrived at Limerick and stormed the defences. The Geraldines acquitted themselves well, and Milo fitz David was left in charge of an Anglo-Norman garrison when the allies withdrew.

By the time that news of Raymond's expedition could reach England, peace had been concluded between Henry II and the High King. Rory's envoys were Archbishop Catholicus ('Cadla') O Duffy of Tuam, the abbot of Clonfert and an individual who styled himself 'Master Laurence' and signed as the Connacht king's chancellor. A key witness was Laurence O Toole, and it is clear that the Irish hierarchy had played a very important role in the drawing up of the so-called Treaty of Windsor formally concluded on 6 October 1175. The terms were in essence that Rory should become Henry's vassal and as such a) hold Connacht directly of the English crown, b) retain a mean overlordship under the English king of those of the Irish who had not Anglo-Norman lords, c) render a tribute in hides both for Connacht and for this overlordship, and d) return to their Anglo-Norman lords those Irish tenants whom their new masters might wish to retain. For his part the English king undertook to make available to Rory military support if his authority should be defied. The intentions of the different parties were clear enough and even commendable, but in modern times the treaty has been universally condemned as unworkable from the outset. In fairness it must be observed that it was the letter and not the spirit that left so many loopholes, and if Rory can fairly be censured for his greedy preoccupation with those clauses that seemed to promise increased authority over his own people, Henry cannot escape blame for his failure to provide much more specific guarantees of the territorial integrity of those parts of Ireland which the Anglo-Normans had still to enter. The fact that the traditional Irish economy was primarily though by no means exclusively pastoral, while the newcomers were interested primarily in arable development, should have made possible a considerable degree of coexistence in a generally underpopulated Leinster and Meath than was in fact achieved. One cannot but be disgusted by the greed with which the invaders seemed almost perversely to prefer often precarious fiefs in the three Irish 'fifths' to exploitation of the full resources of the territory Rory now formally abandoned.

ARDEE   Fortified town

Ardbraccan   Castle

Greencastle

COLERAINE
Mount Sandal

Derry   Killowen

Kilwaughter
Carrickfergus

Caol Uisce

Greencastle

Mag Coba
Dromore   DOWNPATRICK

SLIGO   Clones

Donaghmayne   Dundrum
Newcastle

Ballymote

CARLINGFORD
DUNDALK

Athankip

ARDEE
DROGHEDA

Moydow   Nobber

Dunamon   Granard   Athboy Ardbraccan

Roscommon   Lissardowlan

Ballymoe   Rinndown   Kilbixy   Killallon TRIM Galtrim

Mount Temple   Derrypatrick

Athleague   ATHLONE Horseleap Maynooth   Ratoath

ATHENRY   Ballymore

Moate   Rathwire   Leixlip DUBLIN

GALWAY   Killare Carbury   Castleknock

Loughrea   Meelick

Killeigh   KILDARE Naas

Lorrha   Birr   Geashill

Kinnitty   Castledermot

Roscrea   ATHY

Nenagh   Durrow   CARLOW

Clare Castle Quin   WICKLOW

Bunratty   Bruis   KILKENNY

LIMERICK   Tibberaghny   ARKLOW

Shanid   Kilfeacle

Askeaton   Kilteely   Knockgraffon   Callan

Killeedy   Croom   Kilbolaine   Athassel   Carrick-on-Slaney

Tralee   Ardpatrick   Ardfinnan   WEXFORD

Kilcolman   WATERFORD

Dunloe

Murragh   CORK   YOUGHAL

Ringrone   Imokilly

Timoleague

The approximate location of some of the Anglo-Norman towns and
castles mentioned in the text.

4   Colonial Consolidation

THERE is a little evidence that Henry II, hoping for much from the Treaty of Windsor, genuinely intended at first to honour its provisions. A new bishop of Waterford accompanied the Connacht envoys back to Ireland. The name O Shalvey suggests a local cleric, the consecrators included Laurence O Toole and Catholicus O Duffy, and he was accepted by his flock. Clearly this was no attempt to obtrude an Anglo-Norman on an Irish diocese. The next few months afforded another instance of Henry's good faith. Montmorency, it will be recalled, had been superseded by Raymond le Gros, and was now mischief-making at the English court. It was artfully insinuated that Raymond had wider ambitions than an Angevin king could tolerate, and in the spring of 1176 four commissioners arrived in Ireland, two to serve with Strongbow as political commissars, and two to accompany Raymond back to England. Raymond was preparing to obey when news came that Donal Mór O Brien was besieging Limerick where the small Anglo-Norman garrison was in dire peril. The commissioners themselves authorised Raymond to relieve the city, and he cut his way through an ambush near Cashel and raised the siege. A peace was patched up, too, between Donal Mór and the High King Rory at Lough Derg. Again with the approbation of Henry's commissioners, Raymond next marched into Desmond and rescued Dermot Mac Carthy from his undutiful son Cormac.

Operations were still in progress when a coded letter from Basilia informed him that Strongbow was dead. The news was kept from the Irish as long as possible, and Raymond reached Limerick. It was decided that a garrison so deep in Irish territory might prove a liability, and Limerick was formally consigned to Donal Mór to hold as the king of England's liege. The Normans, though, were not out of sight of the city before O Brien broke down the bridge and set fire to the place.

Strongbow's legal heir was a boy, Gilbert, not yet in his teens, and failing him a girl Isabella of five. Under feudal law the earldom of Leinster passed into the king's hand until the boy should come of age. It was essential that Henry move with speed and decision to ensure that Strongbow's vassals transferred their allegiance to the king, and that the revenues of Strongbow's demesne lands were paid into the treasury. It was also necessary to provide Ireland with a new chief governor at once. The man sent to undertake all these things was fitz Audelm, and he immediately set about the task with a thorough attention that boded ill for the individually ambitious. The Geraldines conspicuously received no favour, particular attention being paid to the hinterland of Dublin. The Leinster lands essentially were held of the king during the minority as they had been held of Strongbow. Donal Cavanagh had been killed in a affray the previous year, and there is no doubt that Maruice fitz Gerald's death also served to make easier fitz Audelm's task. In what is now Kildare the Anglo-Normans were very much in the ascendancy, and two of the three principal lords were sons of Nesta, one of them Geraldine. In the modern Carlow the principal lord was Raymond le Gros, but Irish survival was on a greater scale. In Waterford the eastern end of the modern county was securely in Anglo-Norman possession though the Ostmen were still a force to be recognised. In the present-day counties of

Kilkenny, Laois and Offaly Anglo-Norman lords had obtained a toe-hold and more, while what is now Co. Wexford was Anglo-Norman in the south but mainly in Irish hands in the north. Modern Wicklow was virtually left to the Irish. Ploughland was the one category of swordland with which the Anglo-Normans wished to be enfeoffed, and strategic considerations counted for little once the ports had been secured, and even here one feels that freedom of commercial access rather than military relevance weighed more with the newcomers. The patchwork pattern of settlement was to be an enduring one, and though there was undoubtedly expropriation and even gross injustice, we do well to remember that Strongbow and more recently Raymond le Gros had been able to march against Irish enemies to the west with the support of major contingents of the Leinster Irishry whose loyalty was not normally in question. Donal Mac Gilla Mo-Cholmoc, married to a sister of the widowed Eva, and the occupant of strategic lands between the Liffey and the Wicklow Mountains, was even created a baron. In some cases, though, munificence towards the Church does seem to have cloaked fears that the dispossessed might be in a position to challenge the more arbitrary of the confiscations. In 1174, for example, Henry II had confirmed Strongbow's concession to Hamund Mac Torquil of a portion of his ancestral inheritance, but later in the very same year Strongbow renegued on the agreement and shrewdly gave the land to the always under-endowed Church which could be relied on to defend its title with persistence against all comers.

In the autumn of 1176 fitz Audelm was called on to meet a danger unprecedented where the young colony was concerned, the intervention of Ulster in the affairs of her southern neighbours. In alliance with Murragh O Carroll of Oriel, Malachy Mac Loughlin invaded Meath.

The castle at Slane was overrun and its warden Richard Fleming and many of the garrison killed, while the castles in course of construction at Kells, Galtrim and Derrypatrick, still stockaded mottes and baileys doubtless, were abandoned, and we may suppose that the roads into Dublin once more were choked with refugees. The attack, however, quickly lost momentum, and the Ulster army withdrew. There was civil war in the north of Ulidia, and Malachy's own position among the Mac Loughlins was controversial. As ever, too, relations between the eastern (Tyrone) and western (Donegal) lines of the O Neills were strained. It will be noticed that Rory O Connor held aloof. Unable to bridle his own, he failed equally to come to the support of his new overlord, and Ireland was really in no position to complain if Henry II henceforth regarded the provisions of the Treaty of Windsor a dead letter. Fitz Audelm was not an inspiring leader, and the work of bringing into the king's hand Strongbow's lands cannot have been to the taste of his more independent-minded lieutenants. In February one of these, John de Courcy from Somerset, rode out from Dublin with 300 men and some Irish allies, traversed Meath and Louth, and disappeared into Ulidia. Within a week he was at Dun da Lethglas, now Downpatrick, and putting the captured 'capital' into defensive shape. Rory Mac Dunleavy rallied his levies, but de Courcy won a notable victory. A papal legate happened to be on the scene, one Cardinal Vivian, who had been in Man trying to straighten out the marital affairs of Finuala Mac Loughlin who was wedded to the Manx King, and it is significant that he had condemned the Anglo-Norman irruption even though at that very time on his way to Dublin to affirm Henry II's claim to Ireland. Mac Dunleavy, though, was game for another fall, and appealed to Malachy Mac Loughlin who came to his aid with a massive army. Once again, however, the Irish were unable to withstand the combination of cavalry, mailed men-at arms and archers, and among de Courcy's prisoners were Gilla-in-Coimdhed O Carron primate of Armagh, and Malachy ('Echmilidh'), last native Irish bishop of Down. Both were released with every ostentation, and de Courcy settled down to consolidate an enduring lordship in North Down and South Antrim with major castles at Downpatrick and Carrickfergus.

The success of what had seemed a madcap raid prompted a second expedition from Dublin. This was led by Milo de Cogan who went westwards with 500 men to join Murrough O Connor who had headed a revolt against his own father. The Anglo-Norman force reached Tuam and a detachment burnt Galway, but Rory's adherents pursued a scorched-earth policy which dictated an early withdrawal by the invaders who were continually harassed by guerila-style attacks. The invasion was in the event a complete failure with heavy Anglo-Norman losses, and the luckless Murrough fell into his father's hands and was blinded.

In the meantime two meetings of very different complexions were taking place. In March Cardinal Vivian presided over a synod of the Irish Church convened at Dublin, and solemn excommunication was threatened for any who might seek to deny Henry II's lordship of Ireland. A full publication, too, was at last made of the bull *Laudabiliter*, presumably to demonstrate the consistency of papal policy over the last twenty years. In May Henry II's council meeting at Oxford conferred the lordship of Ireland on the ten-year-old Prince John. His viceroy was to be Hugh de Lacy, fitz Audelm still being responsible for Leinster, and the importance of the Dublin hinterland was once more stressed. De Lacy received Meath on new terms, though the doubling of his knight-service probably reflects nothing more than the enhancement of his resources when he was additionally given special responsibility for Dublin and the mearing with Leinster. On the same occasion, moreover, there was adopted an entirely new policy towards Munster. The hinterland of Waterford was granted to Robert le Poer, Thomond ultimately to Philip de Braose, and Desmond jointly to Robert fitz Stephen and Milo de Cogan. In the event Thomond remained securely in the possession of Donal Mór O Brien, de Braose not being prepared to rise to the challenge, and Dermot Mac Carthy kept three-quarters of his territory by coming to terms with fitz Stephen and de Cogan who had not the resources to exploit more than seven cantreds in the hinterland of Cork. It is interesting, too, that the towns of Cork and Limerick, with the lands immediately dependent on them, were to go to the crown, though only at Cork was the decision implemented. No formal grants were made in respect of Ulster, and Rory O Connor's position in Connacht does seem to have received a measure of *de facto* if not *de jure* recognition.

The years 1178 and 1179 proved relatively uneventful, though in the former, de Courcy appears to have suffered smart defeats when campaigning towards Coleraine and again when raiding into Louth. It was essentially a period of consolidation, and the landscape of great areas of Ireland was being dotted with mottes and with moated manors as the conquerors planted their lands with what tenants they could get. Working generally in favour of the newcomers was a population explosion taking place over most of Western Europe, and from England and Wales and even Flanders there was a steady stream of men glad to take tenancies of good arable land in return for payments that might be in money, services or kind or any combination of the three. Among the native Irish, on the other hand, the same disedifying dissensions continued, aggravated perhaps by the restless wanderings hither and thither of landless men unwilling or unable to come to terms with the new masters of their inheritances. If for a time it looked as though there might be a measure of reconciliation in the north-west between the two lines of the O Neills, in Desmond the fratricidal strife reached new depths of degradation, and characteristic was a sacking of the monastery at Inisfallen near Killarney by a local prince, the detailed description of which recalls the handiwork of the worst type of Norseman.

In 1180 de Courcy married Affrica Godredsdatter, a Manx princess who was also connected by blood or affinity with the Lords of the Isles and the Mac Loughlins. Thirty years previously her father had done homage on behalf of his knight towards whose Ulidian conquests his liege lord was turning a blind eye. More importantly the marriage gave de Courcy access to a fleet, and he was able quietly to build up his position at the mouth of the Bann, though west of the river he seems to have had to depend on smallholder colonists from the Scottish Isles rather than on the more solid and conformist English tenants who appear to have been the backbone of the plantation of the north of Down and the south of Antrim. Emphatically, though, de Courcy's power was confined to Ulidia. When the primatial see of Armagh fell vacant he was in no position to infiltrate a nominee of his own, and the new archbishop was Tomalty O Connor whose connections were with Connacht. This is in marked contrast to the position which obtained in Dublin after the death (14 November 1180) at Eu in Normandy of Laurence O Toole. After months of patient negotiation and pressurisation Henry II was able to procure the election (6 September 1181) of an English monk still not in priest's orders who enjoyed a considerable reputation as a clerk in the king's service. This was John Cumin, and it is again suggestive that he was sent to the pope for consecration (21 March 1182). One cannot fail to remark, too, that by the end of the twelfth century the Angevins had inflicted only three non-Irish bishops on the Irish Church, the other appointments being those for Meath (1192) and Glendaloch (1192). The three dioceses constitute the triangle of the Dublin hinterland which has already been seen to be something of an obsession where Henry II's strategic thinking was concerned. When, moreover, Cumin returned from Velletri it was bearing papal privileges which conflicted with Armagh's traditional primacy, and there can be little doubt that Cumin was not the only Englishman of his day who dreamed of the eventual removal to Dublin of the primatial see. Ironically enough de Courcy was one of those who did most to thwart this design. It suited his interests to have a strong Armagh, and to this end he promoted Patrician devotion with consistent fervour. Most of his coins were to substitute the name of the saint for that of the king, and he was one of the patrons of Jocelin's *Vita Patricii* which contains a neglected but highly significant sequence indicative of Dublin's historic subordination to Armagh.

Later in 1181 Hugh de Lacy fell temporarily from favour, and for a few months he was deprived of his chief governorship in favour of two commissioners sent over from England. Henry may well have been alarmed by an irregular marriage without his permission to a daughter of Rory O Connor, but the political futility of such an alliance would have been clear to all later the same year when the Connacht army, attempting to invade Donegal, was brought to battle in the north of Sligo and utterly overthrown. The upshot was that de Lacy was restored to the justiciarship, though henceforth a minor English cleric was attached to him as a species of political commissar. It was well for the colony that so experienced and resolute a man was at the helm. In 1182 de Cogan was killed in an affray in Desmond, and it needed all the élan of the local commander, Raymond le

Gros, to restore the position. The same year found Donal Mac Loughlin invading Ulidia but being worsted by de Courcy, while Rory O Connor and his son Conor achieved a notable victory over the men of Donegal. Dissension was endemic in the north-west, and had no regard for the realities of life which were that with every day the Anglo-Norman grip on Meath was growing tighter, and a wedge being driven from the Irish Sea towards the Shannon which would make it impossible for any High King to bring North and South together in a great hosting against Dublin. Even inside Connacht, the only province still intact, there was a failure to preserve unity, and in 1183 Rory retired to the monastery at Cong leaving the Kingdom of Connacht to his son Conor. The following year de Lacy once more forfeited Henry II's confidence, and he was replaced on a temporary basis by Philip of Worcester who addressed himself to the important task of edging de Lacy back from the immediate hinterland of Dublin where the Meath mearing was becoming blurred to the earl's and not the crown's advantage. Further to the south-west the treacherous assassination of Art O Melaghlin by an O Brien princeling seems to have relieved the threat of a last-ditch resurgence on the part of the Irish of the Midlands. An attack across the Shannon by Conor O Connor petered out after taking one castle, with the position being more than restored by the construction of a major work at Killare between Mullingar and Athlone. The arrival of Prince John was very much in the air, and it was perhaps to show his own worth that in the early spring of 1185 Philip of Worcester hosted to Armagh where there ensued a curious interlude involving the alleged abdication of Tomalty O Connor from the coarbship of Patrick and the very ephemeral succession of a Louthman, Mael Ísu O Carroll. With a selection of prestigious relics including the *bachall Ísu*, Worcester returned to Dublin to make ready for the approach of Prince John. The stripling Lord of Ireland – he was only seventeen – sailed from Milford Haven on 24 April and arrived at Waterford the next day. He was accompanied by 300 knights and perhaps ten times that number of men-at-arms and archers, and the intention was clearly that he should head an effective governorship of his lordship. A number of Irish Kings came in to make their submission, but were not impressed by his giggling entourage. From Waterford John went to Lismore, then north to cross the Suir at Ardfinnan, and so to Dublin by way of Kildare. He remained in Ireland until just before Christmas, and used his considerable resources to very little purpose. A very small coinage of halfpence with obverse legend IOHANNES: and profile portrait probably relates to his Dublin sojourn. De Lacy seems to have been distant and uncooperative, and John was probably wise to avoid a confrontation with an older man who had the local scene so much at his finger-tips.

The Lord of Ireland's eyes in fact were focussed on the south-west. Rory O Connor had come out from retirement, and had enlisted support from the Anglo-Irish and from Donal Mór O Brien in a bid to displace his son Conor. The west of Connacht was devastated in the war that followed, and Killaloe was burnt in reprisal. Eventually Conor secured recognition as Connacht's king, and in the general turmoil the Anglo-Irish pushed forward into Ossory and the east of Thomond, and castles were begun to command the Suir crossings at Ardfinnan and at Tibberaghny below Carrick-on-Suir, with the odd tactical victory obtained by Donal Mór failing to turn the tide. Again the Irish princes were preoccupied with their own dynastic feudings, while the death of Donal Mac Gilpatrick and murder of Dermot Mac Carthy undoubtedly facilitated Anglo-Norman penetration of Ossory and of Desmond respectively. Donal

Mór blinded another of his brothers, and the murder of Malachy Mac Loughlin by some of de Courcy's men meant that there was now no possibility of intervention from the north where the O Neills were more divided than ever. It was against this background that there was granted to Theobald fitz Walter, the ancestor of the Butlers of Ormonde, a major Shannonside lordship carved out of the north-eastern corner of Thomond. Philip of Worcester was allocated another major lordship centred on the region around Cahir, and William de Burgo a smaller but by no means negligible territory around Athassel between Cashel and Tipperary. These were parchment grants to favourites who would have to cast around for the men and resources to exploit them, but they existed and when the titles came to be tested they would be found good. No less important for the future were confirmations of Naas to William fitz Maurice Fitz Gerald and of the Geraldine lands around Rathmore and Maynooth to his brother Gerald. An absorption of the see of Glendaloch by the archdiocese of Dublin was also approved, but for the time being could not be implemented. For a major hosting against the Irish and for dialogue with the Irish one looks in vain. When John returned to England it was with an empty purse and very little achieved. The justiciarship was not returned to Worcester but given to de Courcy who had been in England and presumably made his peace with Henry II.

John clearly had taken a strong dislike to de Lacy whom his father had already come to distrust, and from the point of view of the English king there was much to be said for de Courcy as justiciar. He had all the prestige that attaches to success, and he occupied a lordship relatively remote from the crucial Dublin hinterland but which directly menaced Meath in the event of de Lacy's interests being diverted from the drive towards the Shannon which constituted the earl's one legitimate ambition. For the moment, too, the pressure was off Ulidia, and de Courcy could turn his attention southwards. Dissensions among the O Neills were more pronounced than ever, and in Donegal royal brother slew royal brother with his own hand. In 1186, too, there were depositions of two of the three remaining province kings, Rory O Connor being finally replaced by his able and ambitious son Conor, and Donal Mac Loughlin by Rory O Laverty who was slain the following year when hosting into Donegal. The great names of the past were thinning out. In 1186 the widowed Dervorgilla withdrew to live out her days in penance at Mellifont, while some years later Raymond le Gros died. Another break with the past was the death around that time of Christian O Conarchy, the former papal legate and, until he resigned in 1179, bishop of Lismore. Undoubtedly the most significant demise at this juncture, though, was that of Hugh de Lacy. The earl had constructed a castle at Durrow with materials from the monastery, and outraged religious susceptibilities and political considerations conspired to bring about his assassination. A young Irishman Gilla-gan-inathair O Mee joined the earl and his friends as they were inspecting the work. De Lacy stooped, and an axe whipped out from under the young lad's cloak decapitated the earl at one blow. In the confusion Gilla-gan-inathair escaped. Henry II is supposed to have heard the news with grim satisfaction, while the burial of head and trunk in the same grave was delayed for twenty years by a disedifying dispute between the Cistercians of Bective and the Augustinians of St Thomas' Abbey, Dublin.

De Lacy's sons were not of age, and so the lands of Meath joined those of Leinster in John's hand. The original design was that he should personally supervise their custody, and it was also proposed that there should follow soon his coronation as King of Ireland, the sanction of Pope Urban III having in fact been obtained, but the death of his older brother Geoffrey caused a complete change of plan. At the time he had received the lordship of Ireland, John had been the fourth surviving son. In 1183, however, his oldest surviving brother Henry had died, and now Geoffrey's demise meant that there was only Richard, still a bachelor and disinclined to matrimony, between him and the Angevin succession. Obviously he had now to be groomed in continental policies, and so his father sent him to France. It fell to his justiciar de Courcy, therefore, to supervise the taking of Meath into his hand, though immediate responsibility was assigned to Philip of Worcester. John, it should be added, appears to have been well content with this arrangement. More than a decade later he still had not woken up to the fact that for him Ireland was a wooden spoon which could turn to silver.

The year 1187 was comparatively uneventful. Rory O Laverty was killed on a Tyrone hosting into Donegal, and Aodh O Rourke, who had made his submission to Rory O Connor only the previous year, led a combined force of the men of Breifne and of Anglo-Norman freebooters on an expedition across Sligo to pillage the monastery at Drumcliff. The following year saw continuing disturbance in Donegal, and de Courcy's Ultonian host marched across Armagh towards Dungannon but was worsted by Donal Mac Loughlin. De Courcy himself hosted into Connacht and turned north to Ballysadare with the intention of falling on Donegal. When, however, it became clear that it would be no walkover, he again changed front but while traversing the Curlew Mountains was attacked by the Connacht army and only extricated himself with difficulty and after suffering heavy losses. Three deaths in 1189 were generally to the advantage of the Anglo-Normans, Murrough O Carroll breathed his last at Mellifont, Donal Mac Loughlin was the victim of Anglo-Norman treachery, and Conor O Connor was murdered by his own household. Either of the two last might well have proved to have been made of the stuff of greatness, and have rallied the Irish, but this was not to be. A fourth death was that of Henry II of England. The constitutional position of Ireland was not affected, but the succession of Richard I in England meant almost complete neglect of Irish affairs where the Crusader monarch was concerned. John's want of genuine interest was nearly as complete, and for the next decade and more the government of the colony was as haphazard as generally successful, a consequence of the essentially pragmatic and undoctrinaire approach of men who were either familiar with the Irish scene or well aware that there was no chance of a massive intervention from England rescuing them from mistakes of inexperience. Before he died Henry II had approved the marriage of the pubescent Leinster heiress Isabella to William Marshal, Earl of Pembroke – her brother had died still a minor a few years previously – and this meant that Strongbow's inheritance passed out of John's custody. The loss of revenue piqued John, and Richard's intervention was necessary before Marshal's position was secure. For nearly twenty years, however, the lord of Leinster was an absentee and took no part in the government of the colony. Two other Normans, on the other hand, now began to be prominent in Irish affairs, Bertram de Verdon and Gilbert Pipard. Favourites of John, they had received extensive grants in Louth, de Verdon around Dundalk and Pipard around Ardee, and O Carroll's death enabled them to begin converting some of the tributary lands into tightly knit fiefs of the conventional Anglo-Norman type. As 'lord of Ulster' de Courcy cannot have been all that happy about this feudalisation of what had been a most useful buffer-state between the colony proper and his remote principality, and it was perhaps to show the flag as much as to obtain booty that we find the Anglo-Normans using a dynastic squabble as a cloak for a reconnaissance in force of Fermanagh, and de Courcy in person hosting to Armagh.

The years 1190 and 1191 were again comparatively uneventful. In the southwest Donal Mór Mac Carthy was able to inflict a sharp defeat on an Anglo-Norman expedition into Desmond, but in Connacht the death of Conor O Connor meant that opposition to the failing Rory crystallised more and more around his still energetic and extremely able younger brother Cathal Crobderg, and in 1191 Rory went to Donegal to seek support. At about this time, too, de Courcy was superseded as justiciar by relative newcomers Peter Pipard and William le Petit who held the office jointly. The supersession must have been galling, but de Courcy could console himself with the reflection that he could now concentrate all his attention on his Ulster lordship. In 1192 legatine status was conferred by Pope Celestine III on Matheus ('Mahon') O Heaney, Cistercian archbishop of Cashel since 1186, a hint perhaps that Tomalty's Armagh primacy was recognised by Rome as somewhat ineffective, and certainly a reflection of papal unease concerning Cumin's ill-concealed ecclesiastical imperialism. In a bid for unity the national synod convened by O Heaney the same year was held at Dublin, and the archbishops of Armagh and Cashel – but not apparently of Tuam – jointly consecrated with Cumin the collegiate church which is now St Patrick's cathedral. Unfortunately little is known of the work of this synod, but it is reasonable to suppose that it endorsed the programme for reform proposed by the decrees of Cumin's own provincial synod of 1186. These had been concerned with the proper administration of the sacraments, the payment of tithe, and the emancipation of benefices from secular control – all matters of

concern to a Church still in process of adopting a paro-
chial structure – and as usual there was a heavy emphasis
on what was still Ireland's besetting sin, widespread
sexual incontinence which found its expression in matrimonial irregularity and clerical concubinage. What
should be stressed, though, is that this licence was by no
means universal. There was always present a strongly
ascetic tradition, and as unsympathetic an observer of
the Irish scene as Giraldus Cambrensis could pay generous
tribute to the exemplary chastity of the run of Irish
priests.

Militarily and politically Munster continued to be the
cockpit of the contest between Anglo-Norman and Gael.
Donal Mór O Brien won a second notable victory near
Thurles, but the ring of castellation was closing in on
Ormond with the construction of major mottes at
Horseleap and Kilbixy in what is now Westmeath and at
Kilfeacle and Knockgraffon in the modern Co. Tipperary.
In 1193 Donal Mór was accused of tolerating the erection
of a third Tipperary castle at Bruis because it menaced
his old Mac Carthy rivals in Desmond, while on the
colony's northern mearing a castle was thrown up at
Donaghmayne in what is now Co. Monaghan. Other
events of the year included the sacking of a monastery
on Lough Ree by Gilbert de Angulo and the death at
Mellifont of Dervorgilla. By now, too, a mint on the
English model had been established at Dublin and was
putting out halfpence and farthings with the names of
prominent citizens who ran the establishment for a share
of the profits. Outside Ireland John had been involved
since 1191 in what became virtually a rebellion with
French support against his brother, but early in 1194
Richard's return to England set the seal on the ignomini-
ous collapse of the whole conspiracy. To de Courcy and
to de Lacy's sons it seemed that John's star had set for
ever, and they committed technical treason by hosting

against Peter Pipard – there is no evidence that Richard ever declared John forfeit of Ireland which in any case was a papal and not a regalian fief. The unfortunate justiciar was taken prisoner, and in a moment of aberration Richard even allowed Walter de Lacy to do him homage for his father's Meath lordship. What had not been bargained for was Richard's extraordinary clemency, and his pardoning of John the following year threatened to put de Courcy and the de Lacy brothers in real jeopardy. As it was, the affair blew over. Walter de Lacy again did homage to John for Meath, while John appointed a new justiciar Hamo de Valognes, a newcomer to the Irish scene. This was in 1195, and in the meantime interest had once more centred on the middle and lower Shannon. The death of Donal Mór O Brien in 1194 opened up Thomond to the Anglo-Normans, and it was not long before Limerick was once more garrisoned by 'grey foreigners'. Gilbert de Angulo led a plundering expedition across the north of Connacht to Assaroe near Ballyshannon, but the booty was small, and Cathal Crobderg O Connor who was now firmly established refused to be distracted from what he rightly believed to be the real menace to Connacht, the Anglo-Normans of Munster. In 1195 he invaded Thomond where the adventurers had blinded Murtagh O Brien, and for a time much seems to have been hoped for from this intervention. A treaty made at Athlone with de Courcy and de Lacy secured his rear, and likewise secured de Courcy's flank when in company with Cathal Crobderg's sons and Rory Mac Dunleavy the Anglo-Normans of Ulster attempted to break out from behind the Bann. Other events of 1195 included a disastrous fire in Dublin which laid low 'the city north of the bridge', and the return to Ireland of Philip of Worcester who, in association with William de Burgo and Theobald fitz Walter, began seriously to colonise Tipperary where Norman influence was to be pronounced throughout the mediaeval period. In 1196 Donal Mac Carthy holding his own in Desmond was able to slight the Anglo-Norman mottes around Imokilly, and successfully sought assistance from Cathal Crobderg who sent a company of archers. The campaign went well, and Donal's forces were all poised to destroy Cork when he was persuaded to spare the city, and what had been a promising counter-offensive petered out. Cathal Crobderg's attention was being diverted by an unsuccessful expedition into Breifne by the Anglo-Normans of Meath which was perhaps inspired by de Burgo to whom John had given a parchment title to Connacht, and who had made a mischievous grant to de Lacy of ten cantreds around Sligo. Another cloud on Cathal Crobderg's horizon was the situation in the far west of Connacht where a major revolt of the O Flahertys was not unconnected with dynastic friction within the O Connors. When, too, Rory Mac Dunleavy attempted to lead a Connacht army against the O Neills he was heavily defeated. The repulse was the more humilitating because de Courcy, after fortifying Mount Sandal to cover Coleraine, was able to host with impunity from Toomebridge to Derry, though one of his lieutenants was beaten off when raiding from the sea, and a raid on Inishowen to some extent miscarried.

In 1197 civil war among the O Briens destroyed the last hope of their maintaining effective power south of the Shannon, and one of Donal Mór's sons, Conor Ruadh, did not scruple to enlist the help of de Burgo against his own brother Donagh. Henceforth Anglo-Norman possession of Limerick itself was assured, and the city received a charter. Within months, too, dies for striking coins were coming down from Dublin where coinage had resumed, and the first moneyer was also the first provost with the Ostman name Siward. The other centres now given the privilege of a mint were Waterford and Carrickfergus, but an attempt to extend it to the non-royal town of Kilkenny was short-lived. Still, the coins struck were halfpence and farthings only, the reason most probably being that Ireland's lord was not the English king who might have viewed with suspicion if not jealousy the striking of pence, the one denomination used in foreign commerce and acceptable for the payment of mercenaries. Significantly in this connection the halfpence and farthings have still to be found outside Ireland. In 1197, too, the Anglo-Normans were able to penetrate West Cork as far as Durrus just south of Bantry. In the following year a castle was begun at Ardpatrick, and the way made open for Anglo-Norman exploitation of the plain of Limerick. In his monastery at Cong, Rory O Connor breathed his last, but a contender to the succession of his brother Cathal Crobderg soon arose in the person of a grandson Cathal Carrach. In the north de Courcy again hosted across Tyrone to Ardstraw and Derry and ravaged Inishowen, but the O Neills both in what is now Co. Donegal and the modern Co. Tyrone were beginning to resolve their dynastic feuds; while in Tyrone there was thrown up a natural leader Aedh O Neill not of the Mac Loughlin line, who took to the sea with five ships, landed near Larne and overran a position probably to be identified with Kilwaughter.

At about this time John replaced Hamo de Valognes as justiciar by Meiler fitz Henry, grandson of Nesta and a veteran of the Anglo-Norman invasion of Ireland. He was to serve John well if deviously for a whole decade. In April 1199 the death of Richard, childless after a late marriage, brought to the English throne the lord of Ireland. This succession has been represented as in some way an usurpation since there was in the background an older brother's son in the person of Arthur of Brittany, but Marshal the absentee lord of Leinster was speaking for the consensus of contemporary opinion when he voiced his personal preference for John. In Munster Hamo de Valognes free of the cares of office could begin work on the great castle at Askeaton, and three sons of Maurice fitz Gerald were assigned important holdings at Shanid, Croom and Kilteely. As the work of castellation proceeded, raids were mounted deep into such territory as remained in Irish possession. It was reported that Munster from the Shannon to the Iveragh Peninsula was laid waste, and certainly devastation on this scale would go far to explain the ease with which the Anglo-Normans occupied the plain of Limerick and overspilled into north Kerry. At Limerick Donagh O Connor was put to death by the Anglo-Normans, and we can see de Burgo emerging as the master-mind of a cynical and cold-blooded conspiracy against Connacht. Cathal Crobderg, however, does not seem to have been intimidated by the death of a nephew who could have been put forward as a puppet rival and he mounted an offensive on the middle Shannon which took the bailey of the castle at Athlone but not the motte itself. In an attempt to come to terms with his nephew Cathal Carrach, too, he made a not ungenerous grant of lands in Connacht which he hoped might assuage his thwarted ambition. In Ulster de Courcy appears to have hosted three times across Tyrone, but on the last occasion Aedh O Neill inflicted a considerable defeat on his army in the neighbourhood of Donaghmore. Beaten back from the heartland of O Neill power, the Ulidian forces, Irish and Anglo-Norman, were next led by Rory Mac Dunleavy on a plundering foray to Armagh.

The year 1200 saw John beginning to take seriously his position as lord of Ireland. Meiler fitz Henry was formally confirmed in his appointment as justiciar and granted substantial territories in what is now north Kerry and in the plain north of Killarney, but written into the new authority was reservation to John himself of the pleas of the crown, some of the more important areas of criminal and civil jurisdiction, and of matters concerning the coinage. His administration, however, had as its first concern the Connacht resurgence under Cathal Crobderg. The Irish crossed the Shannon and hosted deep into Meath, but in their depredations they drew no distinction between colonist and native, and when they withdrew laden with booty the Englishry and Irishry of Westmeath and Longford followed and overran the rearguard. Cathal Crobderg himself had a narrow escape, but unabashed put himself at the head of his main army and hosted towards Kilmacduagh as if against Munster. In reality he intended to destroy his rival Cathal Carrach, but the latter escaped the trap and obtained the intervention of Limerick-based William de Burgo who had a parchment title to Connacht which only awaited an opportunity such as this for its implementation. Cathal Crobderg also sought help from outside Connacht, and procured the support of Aedh O Neill and John de Courcy. In the meantime de Burgo and Cathal Carrach pillaged East Connacht, and from a base established at Athleague extended their devastations to what is now Longford.

The O Neills believed that they were intervening in a dispute confined to Irishmen, and were assured by Cathal Crobderg that they would not be confronted by the Anglo-Norman knights and archers for whom they had acquired a very healthy respect. On this understanding the Ulster forces moved into North Connacht and advanced as far as Roscommon pillaging Sligo on their way. It then became obvious that they were in fact being deployed against de Burgo and his Anglo-Normans, and the O Neill forces in company with the men of Fermanagh withdrew and were harried by Cathal Carrach all the way to Drumcliff. However, de Courcy had Anglo-Normans to pit against de Burgo's mercenaries, and Cathal Crobderg from the point of view of the colonial administration was entitled to this support, while many among the older generation of adventurers must have been anxious to see de Burgo's wings clipped. Accompanied by Hugh de Lacy, de Courcy hosted as far as Kilmacduagh, but in a battle near Tuam was worsted by Cathal Carrach, and it was only with difficulty that the Anglo-Norman lords got their army away to the east and ferried it across Lough Ree. It was a serious blow to the administration especially when a determined attempt was being made to bring some order and unity to the new Anglo-Norman lands in Munster, where most of what is now Co. Limerick but not the city itself and its immediate vicinity was the subject of an overall grant to William de Braose. His new tenantry would include such distinguished names as those of Philip of Worcester, Theobald fitz Walter, Thomas fitz Maurice FitzGerald (scion of the Desmond Geraldines), and William de Burgo himself. The terms were a once-for-all payment of 5,000 marks, a very considerable sum but John was already impecunious, and the service of 60 knights. All this was on parchment only, though, and what still faced the colonial administration in Dublin was the problem of Connacht, a problem made no easier by the fact that John's speculative grants overlapped with conflicts not just between Anglo-Norman and Irish but also between Anglo-Norman and Anglo-Norman. Hugh de Lacy, for example, could produce grants relating to the same lands in Sligo both from de Burgo and from John. A beginning was made to the solution of the problem by finding scapegoats. De Courcy was arrested by Walter de Lacy and imprisoned at Nobber in Louth, while Cathal Crobderg was taken captive to Dublin. Both men were in real jeopardy. There were in de Courcy's past too many incidents which could be construed as treasonable by a hostile court – his 'desertion' of fitz Audelm in 1177 and his attack on John's justiciar in 1194 being perhaps the most obvious – and in 1200 a catalogue of the crowned heads of Europe ending with 'de Courcy kinging it in Ulster' had been the 'jest of the year' at John's Christmas table though a dangerous one where that particular sovereign was concerned. As for Cathal Crobderg, not even the semblance of a trial would be necessary to put him to death. The pages of the Irish annals at this time are littered with references to the assassination, mutilation and capital execution of Irish princes whose only crime was that they stood in the way of the latest ambitions of the Anglo-Norman adventurers. De Courcy was fortunate. Already Meller fitz Henry's consistent advocacy of John's interests was beginning to jar on the tight-knit band of great Anglo-Norman lords whose only wish was to be left alone to exploit individually the enormous tracts of land which lay at their mercy, and de Courcy was personally popular with his own. Walter de Lacy was perhaps not all that sorry that a hosting to Nobber of de Courcy's tenants and their Irish allies gave him a pretext for setting his prisoner free.

With regard to Connacht the council at Dublin decided that Cathal Crobderg was the better option, and perhaps with greater reluctance that de Burgo was the obvious instrument. The latter was instructed, therefore, to drop Cathal Carrach, and did so. Early in 1202 the Munster army headed by de Burgo, and including Irish contingents under the O Brien heirs and the dissident Fineen Mac Carthy, an ex-monk or so it was alleged, hosted into Connacht and reached Boyle. The monastery provided a convenient base and its guest-house was in process of conversion into a fortress when there arrived the news that Cathal Carrach had been killed in a skirmish. De Burgo broke up his camp and quartered his hated mercenaries around the countryside to save the expense of paying them. Cathal Crobderg was solemnly inaugurated at Carnfree, and joined de Burgo at Cong to keep Easter.

Suddenly there went round the countryside like wildfire the rumour that de Burgo too was dead, and with one accord the people massacred their unwelcome guests. Not unnaturally de Burgo rounded on Cathal Crobderg, but he had been alerted and had slipped away. It is possible that many of the more responsible among the Anglo-Normans were not sorry to see the disappearance of a corps of hired thugs interested only in fighting and looting, and no official reprisal was taken against the people of Connacht. De Burgo himself returned to Limerick.

Interest now shifts to the ecclesiastical scene. In 1201 Tomalty O Connor had died, and the primatial see of Armagh was vacant. The 'Irish' candidate was Eugenius ('Echdonn') mac Gilla hUidir and when it became clear that Meiler fitz Henry on John's behalf had other ideas, his election and consecration were rushed through with almost unseemly haste. There were complaints to Rome, and in 1202 Cardinal John of Salerno arrived in Ireland as papal legate. Pope Innocent III's reaction had been that right was on the side of Eugenius, but he left a final decision to his legate. Eugenius had undoubtedly been at fault on certain technicalities, and Rome had no desire to steam-roller an appointment unacceptable to John, but the latter's hands were far from clean. While the debate went on at Rome, Eugenius was declared to be suspended, but he was not deprived. In the meantime the Cardinal presided at a national synod held at Dublin. We have not the decrees, but the remark in the *Annals of Inisfallen* that the Cardinal came 'to reform the men of Ireland' suggests that public morals once more bulked large on the agenda. There were other difficulties. A dispute between an Irish bishop of Lismore and a Norman bishop of Waterford resulted in the former appealing to Rome, and at Tuam there was a purely Irish problem when the family of the dead metropolitan Catholicus

O Duffy attempted to obstruct the succession of an Augustinian abbot Felix ('Felim'?) O Ruane from Saul. Both contests went on for years, and were singularly disedifying. It was also decided to remove the see of Meath from Clonard to Trim, and to enhance its authority by submerging in it Kells on the death of the new occupant. The legate left Ireland in 1203, though, with a new sorrow. A violent quarrel had sprung up between the Archbishop of Dublin and the king over the encroachment of royal forest on church land, and for three years the able and energetic Cumin was an exile from his see.

In 1203, too, de Burgo decided that the time had come for him to begin to implement some at least of his parchment grants of lands to the west of the Shannon. For this purpose he constructed a castle at Meelick characteristically incorporating in the fabric the church. From this base he hosted over the surrounding countryside, and the monasteries of Clonfert and Clonmacnois were not exempt from pillaging. This freelance activity did not commend him to the administration of the colony, and for the moment he and his kind were to be something of an anachronism. When the disturbance included the slighting of the new castle at Limerick by the men of Connacht, the time clearly had come to call a halt, and de Burgo's wings were finally clipped when he was sent over to England to account for his conduct to John himself. In the event he kept his lands, but the custody of the city of Limerick was given to William de Braose whose extensive lands in Thomond would guarantee its security – if de Braose could be persuaded to come over and take possession of them. Further north Gilbert de Angulo raided into Donegal in the hopes of profiting from another dynastic squabble, but his nominee was slain and opportunities for such enterprises were in fact fast ceasing to occur. De Courcy now stood in very bad repute with the administration, and the younger de Lacy was authorised to expel him from his lands. In 1202 de Courcy had been offered a safe conduct to go and make his peace with the king himself but had refused, and now he was paying the price of his contumacy. At Carrickfergus and Down-patrick he had been striking coins in the name of St Patrick, and on some of them his own name appeared as well, and the belated striking of a few halfpence with his king's name and title was still an affront to royal authority as the regalian mints at Dublin, Limerick and Waterford had ceased striking by 1199. Despite the touching fidelity of the de Courcy tenants who offered their sons as hostages if their lord were permitted to go to the king to make his peace, the de Lacy invasion of Ulster was successful. At the same time John was entering into a number of accommodations with surviving Irish princes whereby they received a virtual freehold of part of their territory in return for leasing or ceding the rest to the crown. That the land strictly was not their's to surrender does not seem to have worried either party, but for an Irish prince the arrangement did seem to offer some guarantee against further Anglo-Norman aggression.

John's increasing interest in Ireland is largely explicable as a consequence of the disastrous collapse of his continental interests. At precisely this time the French were over-running the last of the Angevin possessions, and the loss of Normandy impoverished a number of his lords who owned estates both sides of the English Channel and who wished to remain loyal to the English crown. Ireland here gave some room for manoeuvre, but even more important was the potentiality of the lordship where John's personal prestige and resources were concerned. He took, therefore, a number of steps designed to con-solidate the position of the crown. In 1204, for example, he ordered that all his writs were to run in Ireland just as they did in England, and particularly important because they conferred jurisdiction in all cases of land-title were those of *Mort d'ancestre* and *Breve de Recto* which were made retrospective to 1172, and *Novel disseissin* retrospective to April 1199. It was also laid down that after Michaelmas 1205 it would be no defence to a criminal prosecution that the victim of the crime was Irish, and John clearly envisaged the extension of English law to all the native Irish as and when the opportunity offered. His Anglo-Norman subjects, though, were of another mind, and one of the ironies of Irish history is that by the time the Crown had overcome their opposition, the native Irish were no longer interested, while the erstwhile oppressors themselves were beginning to prefer Irish customary law. At a more practical level the year 1204 is important because John ordered the construction of Dublin Castle as a secure place in which to house the Irish treasury. Large sums were beginning to accrue from the royal revenues, and it was important that they should be in safe keeping pending their dispatch across the Irish Sea. At about this time, too, a new coinage began to be issued. It was under the control of a royal civil servant, Robert of Bedford, who was later pensioned off with the see of Lismore, and at first was struck only at Dublin. Some halfpence and farthings were put out to meet local needs, but most of the coins were pennies. These were identical in weight and fineness with English pence, and most were shipped to England to finance John's Continental wars.

Militarily 1204, a year of pestilence, was notable for a victory achieved by Donal Mac Carthy over the Anglo-Normans attempting to force their way through the pass at Redchair in the Ballyhoura Mountains. In the north de Courcy returned to Ulidia, but was taken prisoner by Hugh de Lacy, and it was alleged that he only secured his freedom by pledging himself to go on the Crusade. It may be, though, that de Lacy feared that his opponent would be pardoned by John, and wished to give him more rope to hang himself. De Courcy in fact entered into alliances with the Scotto-Norse of the Isles and with Aedh O Neill, and John was moved at last to grant to Hugh de Lacy the earldom of Ulster (29 May 1205). When de Courcy came with his Norse fleet to besiege Dundrum, Walter de Lacy marched to his brother's support, and de Courcy eventually admitted defeat. There could now be no question of his being reinstated, but it is significant that he seems to have retained his English properties, and that in 1219 his widow's dower-lands west of the Bann were identifiable and respected. A few months later occurred the death of William de Burgo who like so many others had been involved in controversy with the increasingly officious Meiler fitz Henry. His son was a minor, and his estates passed into John's hand, as did those of Theobald fitz Walter who died early in 1206 likewise without adult heir. Other deaths in 1206 were those of Matheus O Heaney, archbishop of Cashel, and of the resolute Donal Mac Carthy, and in both cases the succession was disputed. Fortunately the Armagh dispute had been resolved with the primatial authority of Eugenius loyally accepted by the English of Meath when he presided at a synod held near Mullingar early in 1205; and at Cashel, where John put forward a candidate of his own, as it happens an Irish Cistercian Ailbe O Mulvey, the issue was not pressed, and Donatus ('Donagh') O Lonergan was eventually elected by due if leisurely process. In Desmond, on the other hand, the short-lived usurpation of Fineen Mac Carthy proved disastrous, and the position was not restored by his expulsion. Already in 1206 the Anglo-Normans had erected a castle at Cork, and now in 1207 one was built at Dunloe near Killarney to protect the colonists pouring into the basin of the Laune and Maine.

John's desire to consolidate his authority over Ireland is well seen in 1207. The previous year had seen an embarrassing visit to him in England by Archbishop Eugenius who was able to point to the injustices perpetrated on the Irish by Anglo-Norman lords, and the king was probably not sorry to have a pretext for bridling their power. Reserved now to the royal justices in Ireland were all cases involving the equivalent of freehold tenure as well as the so-called pleas of the crown. These were specified in new grants early in 1208 to Walter de Lacy and to William Marshal of Meath and Leinster respectively, grants which removed certain ambiguities but which certainly defined much more closely the rights and duties of the grantees. The reserved pleas of the crown brought within the jurisdiction of the royal justices all cases of rape, arson, treasure trove and forestalling (armed resistance to royal officers). Rape was of particular significance in a feudal society preoccupied with legitimacy, and arson was peculiarly reprehensible where towns of largely wooden construction were of cardinal importance as centres of opposition to encroachment by native Irish and new feudal magnate alike. Side by side with the grants of lands to military adventurers had gone the incorporation of a large number of towns where humbler individuals could enjoy the fruits of their skill and enterprise. Burgess status was eagerly sought after, and the model usually taken when granting these corporate rights was Breteuil in Normandy. Treasure trove was a traditional regalian privilege, but was probably now written in because of John's increasing financial embarassment as he came to depend in his continental campaigns more and more on mercenaries and less and less on his increasingly un-cooperative feudal host. The soil of Ireland was rich in buried gold ornaments, and at least as early as 1215 the breaking of much new ground for ploughing and in the course of throwing up of mottes and ramparts led to John exercising his rights, the first recorded instance relating to treasure found at Killallon near the Meath/Westmeath mearing.

As early as 1205 Cathal Crobderg had agreed in principle to cede John two cantreds west of the Shannon in return for full recognition of his kingship of Connacht, one third of which he was to hold in fee and two-thirds subject to tribute. The total annual cost on both accounts was the very moderate one of 400 marks, and in 1207 tenancies of the two cantreds in Roscommon were granted to John Marshal and to Gilbert de Angulo, so that Cathal Crobderg could congratulate himself that there were now responsible Anglo-Normans interested in ensuring that their own position was not threatened by further Anglo-Norman expansion across the Shannon. Connacht, moreover, was insulated to some extent from the very serious internal quarrels of the colony which lasted from 1201 until John intervened personally in 1210. Meiler fitz Henry had become increasingly unpopular as a consequence of his taking into the king's hand of the de Burgo and fitz Walter lands, while the duplicity in his dealings with the absent William de Braose in the matter of Limerick gave further cause for anxiety as well as offence. He had now gone out of his way to pick a quarrel with the returned William Marshal, and many of the Anglo-Irish lords must have begun to wonder where it would all end. Marshal himself was the soul of prudence and loyalty, but the de Lacy brothers took the law into their own hands and in 1207 laid successful siege to fitz Henry's great new motte at Horseleap. The dissension between their masters encouraged the Irish of the Offaly-Tipperary mearing to rise, and Murtagh O Brien of Slieve Bloom, a cousin of the puppet king of Thomond, and Cormac O Melaghlin obtained a number of successes. The new castles at Lorrha, Birr and Kinnitty were over-run, but quarrels within the O Melaghlins in particular, proved the undoing of the Irish, though Art was still in the field as late as 1214. In the autumn of 1207 Meiler fitz Henry had gone to John in England to denounce both de Braose and William Marshal, but he seems to have overplayed his hand, and by March of 1208 it was clear that his days as justiciar were numbered. Before the end of the year John had appointed in his place the Earl of Ulster, Hugh de Lacy, and fitz Henry had had to come to terms with his old adversaries. De Lacy's appointment, though, was only temporary, and by the end of the year Ireland was ruled on John's behalf by John de Grey, Bishop of Norwich. A new situation had arisen with the arrival in Ireland of the absentee William de Braose who had finally fallen out with John and even hinted that there were disclosures he could make about the fate of Arthur of Brittany. De Braose went first to William Marshal who was technically a vassal of his, and then to his son-in-law Walter de Lacy. John de Grey might fulminate, but the sympathy of the Anglo-Normans in Ireland was with de Braose, and the king had to bide his time. During 1209 little of importance occurred, though continuing disturbance in Donegal contributed significantly to the emergence there of the O Donnell dynasty, while in Desmond the notorious Fineen Mac Carthy was slain by the O Sullivans after a piratical raid on Iveragh.

The spring of 1210 saw John preparing to come himself to Ireland to winkle out William de Braose. He assembled a fleet and army at Milford Haven, and on 20 June disembarked just outside Waterford where John de Grey was waiting for him. Donagh O Brien was confirmed as king of Thomond and granted the lordship of Carrigogunnel, but his older brother Murtagh Finn was taken off in the royal entourage as a hint that there were alternative candidates if Donagh should misbehave. By 21 June John was at New Ross, and the next day at Kilkenny, the *caput* of Marshal's earldom, where he stayed for three days. The earl had accompanied the king from England, and his loyalty could not be faulted. On 26 June the king was in Naas, and two days later in Dublin, and Walter de Lacy was seeking terms. The king was implacable and hosted across Meath to receive the piece-meal submissions of de Lacy's more prudent tenants. On 30 June he was halfway to Trim where he arrived on 2 July and stayed two nights. He moved north to Ardbraccan where he was joined by Cathal Crobderg, and on 7 July was sleeping in the royal castle at Louth. The next day he was in Dundalk, and Hugh de Lacy fell back before him burning his castles before they could fall into his hands. Nicholas de Verdon submitted, and the generous treatment accorded him completed the rot that had already set in where the de Lacy vassalage was concerned, so that John's army advanced northwards swollen with contingents from Meath and Louth. He was at Carlingford on 9 July, and neatly avoided the possibility of having to force the passes of the Mournes by shipping part of his army to Ardglass while the remainder went across a bridge of boats at Narrow Water. Dundrum was thus outflanked, and Downpatrick surrendered. The last stand was made at Carrickfergus, but after a siege of nine days the great castle fell on 28 July. Hugh de Lacy got away, and one of de Braose's two young sons. The other with his mother was intercepted by Duncan of Galloway, Affrica's kinsman, who was gleefully assisting in the downfall of the de Lacy brothers who had pulled down de Courcy who himself accompanied John's expedition and brought the prisoners to the king. Maud de Braose and her son later were starved to death at Windsor. William de Braose himself and Walter de Lacy were at large and remained so. The former died in France the next year, while the latter eventually was given back his earldom. For the moment, though, John's triumph was complete, and immediately masons and carpenters were set to work to get back into shape the stone castles at Carrickfergus, Dundrum and Carlingford which were to be garrisoned for the English king. Two galleys were ordered to be built at Antrim for service on Lough Neagh

– Aedh O Neill almost alone of the Irish princes refused to give hostages – and on 28 July John began his journey south. On 2 August he was at Downpatrick, and three days later he had reached Carlingford by way of Hilltown and Narrow Water. An expedition was sent off to the Isle of Man, and the main army passed through Drogheds, Duleek, Kells and Fore to reach Granard on 12 August. Two days later the king had an angry interview at Rathwire with Cathal Crobderg who had returned from Connacht without his son as hostage, and John had to make do with four prominent members of Cathal's household who were forced to accompany John back to England. On 18 August John was in Dublin, and six days later he sailed for home. It had been a whirlwind campaign, and it owed its success to the utter fidelity of one man. Had William Marshal not set an example of loyalty at the outset, John's Irish vassals might well have bound themselves into a conspiracy behind the wronged de Braose and destroyed the royal army. Typically, though, one of John's last acts on Irish soil had been grossly to humiliate his truest servant by demanding hostages not only from him but from his vassals.

No sooner was John out of Ireland than Cathal Crobderg came to terms with John de Grey who had advanced to Athlone and built a new castle covering the reconstructed bridge. It was a stone castle, and perhaps because of unconsolidated earthworks lying beneath it part of it was to collapse the following year. In the meantime Geoffrey de Marisco, Archbishop Cumin's nephew, and Donagh O Brien had hosted northwards from Limerick through Tuam and into Mayo. Cathal Crobderg gave the required hostage, and the following year his followers were duly returned from England. In 1211 there was renewed war among the Irish of Connacht, and the Scotto-Norsemen plundered near Derry where they shared avidly in the continuing dynastic troubles of

Donegal. While de Grey was in England, the office of justiciar was occupied by William le Petit who had been one of Walter de Lacy's vain embassy to Dublin in the last days of June 1210, a measure of how effectively John's intervention had broken de Lacy's power. In 1212 there was renewed civil war in Desmond, but de Grey's eyes were fixed on the north. Gilbert de Angulo was charged with building a castle at Caol Uisce near Castle Caldwell at the western outlet of Lough Erne, and another was begun at Clones. The men of Fermanagh, however, fought back, and further south de Grey's household troops experienced a humiliating reverse at the hands of Cormac O Melaghlin in the course of which the justiciar's baggage-train and pay-chest were looted. What heartened the English king, though, was a declaration of loyalty organised by the faithful William Marshal and subscribed to by most of the great Anglo-Norman lords resident in Ireland. John was by now involved in a dispute with the papacy, and this gesture of support was as exceptional as welcome. Towards the end of the year came the news of the death of John Cumin, but the English king had little difficulty in filling the metropolitan see of Dublin with another English nominee, Henry of London, like his predecessor an experienced and able administrator. In 1213, though, John's troubles in England reached a new peak, and de Grey rendered signal service when he brought 500 knights to Barham Down in Kent where John was mobilising his forces to repel a threatened invasion from France. In his absence Geoffrey de Marisco headed the administration, but when de Grey was re-tained in England a more permanent arrangement gave the justiciarship to Henry of London. It was doubtless preoccupation with events in England that explains a number of Irish successes in this year. Caol Uisce was captured, and de Angulo killed, while Aedh O Neill not only stormed Clones but burnt Carlingford. The colonists, however, achieved more enduring successes with a victory over O Brien of Slieve Bloom at Killeigh, near Tullamore, and the building of castles at Roscrea and Coleraine, the last a Scotto-Norse foundation and part of the deliberate English policy of settling colonists from the Isles between what is now Co. Tyrone and the sea. By 1214 the administration in Dublin was once more in full control. Cormac O Melaghlin was worsted, and his attacks on Athboy and Birr took only the baileys and not the mottes or keeps themselves. The Anglo-Norman castles at Birr, Durrow and Kinnitty were refurbished, and a motte thrown up beside the monastery at Clonmacnois. Civil war continued in Desmond, but in Ulster Aedh O Neill was able to obtain yet another victory over the Anglo-Normans in Ulidia, a success the more valuable because the coastline from Larne around to Derry was being systematically granted away to the Scotto-Norse who in 1215 extended their operations to Inishowen. Basically, however, the dynastic conflicts that had been the curse of Ulster since the waning of Mac Loughlin power half a century before were now resolved. In what is now Tyrone Aedh O Neill was firmly in the saddle, and in Donegal the O Donnells. For the time being, too, the Irish of Ulster were prepared to sink their differences. In July 1215 Geoffrey de Marisco replaced Henry of London as justiciar, and in September of the same year he negotiated a final settlement with Cathal Crobderg O Connor. The Shannon was constituted the frontier, and the two cantreds in Roscommon restored to Connacht. The castle of Athlone, though, was to remain in the keeping of the English crown, and the annual render for Connacht was to be 300 marks, the whole kingdom now being held in fee. Only the English king's coarb could dispossess Cathal Crobderg of all or any of his lands, and so at one stroke Cathal was secured against his own kindred and Anglo-Norman adventurers. All this was guaranteed by a formal charter for which the Connacht king had to pay 5,000 marks. It was a reasonable settlement, but Connacht's acceptance was ensured by blackmail. Drawn up on the same occasion and its content doubtless leaked to Cathal Crobderg was a second charter which would have given young Richard de Burgo all the rights in Connacht that had been granted to his father. It was not meant to be implemented, but the menace was there, and Cathal Crobderg very wisely put his name to what has come to be known as the Peace of Athlone. He was an anachronism, but a year later a happening in Tuam showed how wedded was Connacht to the Irish past. It will be remembered how the O Duffy family had resented the consecration of an O Ruane as archbishop in 1202. In 1216 Felix was the victim of a brutal assault, temporarily imprisoned and even manacled. Old traditions of hereditary coarbship died hard, and how remote Connacht was from the rest of Ireland is indicated by the circumstance that the outrage was possible despite the clear warning given some twelve years earlier. Then Bishop Robert of Waterford threw away his case and forfeited papal sympathy by laying hands on his unfortunate brother of Lismore and personally supervising his physical chastisement. Not only had Robert died excommunicate, but Innocent III himself had intervened to ensure that the sentence was promulgated and 'Malachias', a Cistercian, restored to his see.

John has not generally been the subject of a favourable verdict from historians, but it must be conceded that in Ireland he had bridled the rapacity of the Anglo-Norman adventurers. He had laid the foundations of a government that was alien but preferable surely to the no less alien rule than would have ensued if matters had been allowed to drift. On the other hand, the degree of relative efficiency he conferred on that government may well be thought fundamental to the fact that the Dublin Castle he commanded to be built was still the seat of the English government of Ireland seven hundred years later. If to some extent he cheated the Anglo-Normans of their prey, they were among the most loyal of his subjects when disaffection was rife during the last years of his reign. If, on the other hand, the native Irish hoped for more from him that they in the event received, he in fact ensured that they would not be the victims of policies which hovered on the brink of genocide. It is noticeable and significant how little the Irish annalists have to say of events in Ireland under the year 1216 in the October of which he died. Strong government is of its nature uneventful. John's successor was Henry III, a boy of nine, and the regent named by the father on his deathbed the much-tried but still faithful William Marshal.

5 The Doldrums

THAT Henry III survived to attain his majority was due in no small part to the integrity of William Marshal. Although the regent had in fact only three years to live, in England they were years of crisis in the course of which a French army had to be shepherded off English soil. In Ireland they were surprisingly uneventful. Walter de Lacy proved generally co-operative, and what trouble there was centred on his half-brother William who in 1215 had begun to look after Walter's interests in Meath but who was now addressing himself to Hugh de Lacy's forfeited earldom of Ulster. In 1217, for example, he had to be ordered to restore to the crown the castles of Dundrum and Carlingford, and it must seem likely that his was the disruptive influence that had prompted yet another Anglo-Norman raid on Armagh which ended ingloriously when the plunderers were pursued and chastised by Aedh O Neill. At Armagh the death of Echdonn late in 1216 had led to an interesting situation when the chapter had had the prescience to anticipate the king's licence to proceed to an election by choosing their dean, the Englishman Luke Netterville. It was a move in fact in the 'Irish' interest, for the election of an Irishman, even if it could have been procured, would doubtless have encouraged the pretensions of Dublin. As it was, the regency had to accept the situation, and racialist advantage was neatly negatived when the primacy of Armagh came up for discussion. In 1217 there was an illustration of the dangers of the position when Geoffrey de Marisco attempted to obtrude a kinsman Robert Travers on the see of Killaloe. The same year saw the construction of a castle there, presumably to overawe the chapter as much as to cover the Shannon crossing, but an appeal to Rome on behalf of the canonically elected Donatus ('Donal') O Heaney ultimately proved successful. In 1216, on the other hand, there was grave scandal within the Cistercian order which now had a total of 34 houses in Ireland. The majority had been founded by Irish initiatives, and of these most were either daughters or grand-daughters of Mellifont. They had developed a very characteristically Irish version of Cistercian spirituality, and it was natural that Cîteaux should be concerned. Unfortunate, though, was a rather heavy-handed attempt to impose uniformity, and this exacerbated existing racial tensions, so that the general chapter of 1216 was treated to a catalogue of enormities which included the deployment of armed levies against the Clairvaux visitors at Mellifont and Jerpoint. Generally, though, the Irish houses did accept even if under protest the general chapter's authority, and for a time it seemed that the affair might blow over with the successful imposition of new abbots on the two monasteries most deeply implicated.

An interesting sidelight on the nascent Anglo-Irish economy is afforded by an incident of the Manx herring-fishery in 1217. The crews of the entire Irish fishing-fleet swarmed ashore in a sensational affray, and it is recorded that they had come from the coastline from Derry round to Waterford. In the same year, too, Geoffrey de Marisco's financial methods led to a tightening up of procedures in respect of the royal revenues, and all rents and fines were now supposed to pass through the royal exchequer. The English monarchy was under heavy financial strain, and Ireland had not yet become the burden on the English exchequer that it was to be from the fourteenth century onwards. That these debts to the crown were still being claimed and paid is, of course, an indication that there was effective government over large areas of the colony, and this acceptance of royal authority undoubtedly owed much to a gesture made in February 1217 when the revised provisions of Magna Carta were specifically extended to Ireland. Magna Carta had been thought of as a baronial victory over royal absolutism, and the re-issue gave the Anglo-Normans a feeling of security of tenure even if in reality the protection was largely artificial.

In 1218 the major events were a hosting across Tertry by the Ulidian Anglo-Normans which resulted in the deaths of two of the Bannside Irish princes, and a further rebuke to de Marisco concerning the finances. The administration continued on an even keel, and it is very noticeable that in 1219 Richard de Burgo found a frosty reception for his proposal that he should be allowed to purchase a new edition of the 1215 alternative grant of Connacht. The restraint is the more remarkable since Cathal Crobderg O Connor was having his difficulties with his Irish subjects and neighbours. In 1219, for example, Murrough O Farrell had invaded his kingdom from the northeast, and in 1220 some internal conspiracy seems to lie behind the summary execution of Dubhdara O Malley. Although, then, the death of William Marshal in 1219 meant an accretion of power to Hubert de Burgo, the English justiciar and Richard's uncle, the boat was not rocked, and no encouragement was given to Cathal Crobderg's enemies. In the southwest Dermot Mac Carthy took the castle at Timoleague, and it is clear that the Irish of South Kerry and West Cork still were able to give a good account of themselves. Administratively an exchequer on the English model was beginning to get into its stride, and a further indication of the fundamental importance of Dublin for the colony was the 1219 elevation of Cumin's collegiate church of St Patrick to cathedral status.

In 1220 there was a final tidying up of loose ends left over from the restoration of Meath to Walter de Lacy. It was agreed, for example, that Drogheda should be ceded to the Crown, but compensation was paid. The earl was now free to pursue an expansionist policy on the Cavan mearing, and overran the O Reilly crannog on Lough Oughter. Further south Murrough O Farrell had shifted operations to Longford, and an O Connor and an Anglo-Norman jointly headed the retaliatory expedition. The northwestern march of Meath seems to have been particularly sensitive at this juncture because of the emergence of a strong O Donnell dynasty in Donegal which was seeking to impose its overlordship on a weakened Breifne. Other events of this year included the death of Meiler Fitz Henry in the monastery to which he had retired at the end of John's reign; an unequivocal condemnation from Pope Honorius III of the 1216 or 1217 declaration that no Irishman was henceforth to be made a bishop, and the termination of Henry of London's papal legateship. Fresh attempts were made, moreover, to bring some order to de Marisco's tangled accounts, and by now it must have begun to be clear to all that peculation and not incompetence lay at the root of the matter. When the following year he was superseded as justiciar it was by that experienced and incorruptible administrator Henry of London, and it is significant that earlier in the year he had not been allowed to redeem himself by a successful hosting into West Cork which resulted in the construction of a castle at Murragh between Bandon and Dunmanway. Walter de Lacy was also on the offensive but an attempt to force the Shannon and build a castle at Athleague misfired when Cathal Crobderg O Connor retaliated with an expedition into Longford. During the same year Ireland was graced by the visit of an Italian cardinal as papal legate, James the Penitentiary, and there is a reminder of the way papal finances were being put on a new footing at precisely this period in the Irish annalist's complaint that the cardinal left with 'horseloads of gold and silver from the clergy of Ireland'. There could also have been mentioned, one feels, the definitive consecration to Killaloe of Donatus O Heaney in the place of Robert Travers.

Metrologically stormy, the year 1222 seems to have been remarkably uneventful on the political front, though the shadow of Hugh de Lacy loomed large. Ulster was garrisoned against him by the smoothly efficient Henry of London, and when in 1223 he arrived in Ireland it was to join his turbulent half-brother William in Meath. The two men proceeded in an attempt to blackmail the Dublin administration into conceding Hugh's claims by a systematic harrying of the Midlands, and Henry of London may even have had to buy peace for money. In Connacht the position of the elderly Cathal Crobderg O Connor was again threatened, and his nephew Dermot was slain by the king of Galloway when attempting to collect forces for a coup against his uncle. The construction of an island-fortress by William de Lacy at an unknown point on the Cavan/Westmeath mearing again provoked a strong reaction from Connacht, and the crannog was carried and the local levies in the garrison dismissed to their homes on parole. Another notorious trouble-maker in the Leinster march had been Murrough O Farrell, but he fell in an affray with a kins-man, and Cathal Crobderg's last major concern seems to have been a scandal in the area of Kilmacduagh where a local prince had been slain when under the protection of the Church.

On 28 May 1224 the king of Connacht breathed his last. He had been true to his promises to the Dublin administration, and only a few weeks before his death he had denounced Hugh de Lacy and warned that the fidelity of others was suspect. His reasonable expectation was that his son Aedh should succeed him on much the same terms, but some of his brothers had other ideas. In the meantime William de Lacy was making mischief in Breifne, and Hugh de Lacy had joined with Aedh O Neill and was happily breaking up the Scotto-Norse plantations along the coasts of Derry and Antrim. The castle at Coleraine was taken, and the work of John's closing years very largely undone. To meet the crisis it was decided to employ Walter de Lacy to reduce to obedience his own lordship of Meath, and to send over to Ireland William Marshal the younger. He arrived at Waterford, and soon afterwards took over as justiciar from Henry of London. With Walter de Lacy he marched on Trim where a number of dissidents had taken the castle. After a siege of five weeks they surrendered, and the pacification of Meath could then proceed apace. The situation in Ulster was more complex, with Hugh de Lacy ravaging the de Verdon lands in Louth, but the dispatch of a small force by water sufficed to bring about the raising of the siege of Carrickfergus. Hugh de Lacy went inland to Aedh O Neill, and by October the situation had been transformed. Earlier that year Aedh O Connor had attempted to whip up support for his kingship among the more militant of his subjects by hosting into Longford and taking the castle at Lissardowlan, but as soon as English royal authority became effective once more, and the victims able to appeal to their lord, he withdrew beyond the Shannon and reverted to his traditional alliance. Further north William de Lacy was a fugitive among the Irish, and his mother, wife and children prisoners, after the O Reillys had switched their allegiance and joined the Crown forces in an attack on their old island-fortress on Lough Oughter. Concentrated at Dundalk and poised for an attack on Ulster was a major hosting of the colony and its Irish allies, and it says much for Aedh O Neill's coolness that he prepared to hold the

Moyry Pass against all comers. At this moment, though, Hugh de Lacy lost his nerve, and the good standing with the Crown of his brother Walter proved his salvation. Negotiations were set in train which resulted in Hugh de Lacy surrendering to William Marshal against some understanding that matters would be arranged to meet his legitimate claims. No attempt was made to force the Gap of the North, and the opposing armies broke up and dispersed to their homes. It had been made very clear that the ultimate loyalty of the Anglo-Norman was to his own class.

Aedh O Neill for his part had no intention of lying low, and in the spring of 1225 invaded Connacht where Cathal Crobderg's brothers were plotting the overthrow of their nephew Aedh. His intervention was decisive, and Rory's son Turlough was taken in triumph to Carnfree and solemnly inaugurated as king of Connacht. It seems to have been a popular development, but in the circumstances prevailing in Ireland at that time dissension was midsummer madness. William de Burgo's son Richard, Hubert de Burgo's nephew, had been biding his time, and in May 1225 he was appointed seneschal of Munster. The very success of the coup was its undoing. Turlough and his brothers appear to have been unwilling to take Aedh O Neill into their confidence, and he betook himself home. In the meantime the dispossessed Aedh O Connor went to Athlone where many of the Anglo-Norman lords had met to discuss matters of mutual concern, and soon returned with the acting justiciar, Geoffrey de Marisco, and a feudal hosting which included Irishry from Thomond and Westmeath. A second column also entered Connacht from the south, and one can understand that Aedh was not in the least pleased with this intervention of an army which he could not accompany. The strategy of his uncles, on the other hand, was to fall back before the invaders and hope in the end they would weary of the war. Considerable devastation was wrought though there was remarkably little serious fighting, Aedh was brought to Tuam, and the Anglo-Normans withdrew. The Connacht king's triumph seemed complete but in fact his position was considerably weakened as his allies insisted on taking hostages from among his supporters to secure the payment of their wages. Within weeks Aedh was back among the Anglo-Normans to seek a second intervention, and they for their part had no objection to a species of fighting that promised good pay for little risk. There was more marching and countermarching, a little skirmishing, and eventually Aedh's uncles were driven out of a ruined countryside, one at least taking refuge with Aedh O Neill. Pestilence stalked the land, and the victory proved as hollow and ephemeral as any in the whole course of Irish history.

In 1226 purely English politics once again impinged directly on the Irish scene. It was the heyday of Hubert de Burgo, and William Marshal's power and influence could not but arouse the jealousy of the English justiciar who had had to play second fiddle to his father during the critical years 1216-19. In June the not too scrupulous Geoffrey de Marisco was once again appointed justiciar, and Aedh O Connor was summoned to Dublin to surrender a Connacht forfeit by his father as well as himself – the reference to the alternative instrument of 1215 is unmistakeable. The beneficiary, needless to say, was to be Richard de Burgo who was to hold Connacht for an annual rent of 300 marks (500 after 1231) saving the five Roscommon cantreds opposite Longford and Carrick-on-Shannon which were to go to the Crown. De Burgo cannot have had the resources to exploit the province, and the hope doubtless was that whoever emerged as least weak among the O Connors would strike his own bargain with de Burgo and hold of him the leavings. It is to the credit of William Marshal, in England too a consistent opponent of royal absolutism, that he refused to implement this cynical betrayal of an old companion-in-arms, and this cost him his justiciarship. Later a tale was current that he had had to rescue Aedh at the sword-point from out of the council-chamber in Dublin, but the truth appears to be that Aedh and de Marisco met at Athlone, that there was an affray, and that Aedh escaped. In the skirmish at least one high-ranking Anglo-Norman was killed, and part of Athlone burnt, and this of course played into de Burgo's hands. In the meantime Ireland, Gaelic as well as Anglo-Norman, was afforded a new illustration of her incorporation in the European polity. For the first time the papacy consented to the imposition of a royal tax on the clergy, the so-called 'clerical tenth' in theory voluntary and on this occasion in practice nominal. It was part of the price that the Irish Church was having to pay for fairly effective papal intervention against the cruder manifestations of English political ascendancy. In 1223 the sees of Ferns and Kildare, and in 1224 Limerick, had passed to Englishmen, but in the latter year Honorius III had again condemned the proposition that Irishmen should be disqualified from election or nomination to major benefices, and in 1225 the translation of Marianus ('Mairin') O Brien from Cork to Cashel was a significant defeat for Henry of London's policies. The arrival of the Dominicans in Ireland at Dublin and Drogheda in 1224 provided an interesting new ingredient for the ecclesiastical hotch-potch. The Franciscans arrived first at Youghal in 1231 or 1232. Their provenance too was English, but both orders assimilated well into the Irish scene, and were to some extent a counterpoise to the influence of the new English-style chapters. It was, however, the good sense and timing of the chapter of Armagh which obtained the succession of an Irishman Donatus ('Donnchad'?) O Furey by translation from Clogher in 1227 when the primatial see fell vacant with the death of Netterville.

Aedh O Connor's escape from the trap at Athlone was followed by his public forfeiture of his kingdom, and the award of Connacht to de Burgo. A quisling also called Aedh was quickly found from among the deposed king's uncles, and accompanied de Burgo on an expedition which struck deep into the new Anglo-Norman lordship and reached Lough Mask. A second expedition by de Marisco led to the construction of a castle at Rinndown and another at Athleague, and from Meath there was a further overspill of Anglo-Normans and tame Irishry who plundered Mayo and Sligo. The dispossessed Aedh took refuge in Donegal, but later treated with de Marisco who was not perhaps all that sorry to have his own tame O Connor as a potential rival to de Burgo's. De Marisco's days as justiciar in fact were numbered, and in February 1228 he was superseded by Richard de Burgo. In the same year the original Aedh was murdered in de Marisco's own house by a jealous English carpenter who had misunderstood Irish customs and who was promptly strung up for his pains, while the rival Aedh was hosted in triumph to Carnfree and inaugurated as a Gaelic king the vassal of an Anglo-Norman lord. The main focus of interest, however, shifts to Mellifont where a special visitation was carried out on behalf of the general chapter by Stephen of Lexington, coincidentally but not very tactfully an Englishman.

From the first there had been in Irish Cistercianism a clash of two temperaments, the Irish and the European. The arrival in Ireland of the Anglo-Normans had exacerbated this, even though there was a quite surprising degree of co-operation between representatives of the two traditions. Foundations from Mellifont had been made by genuinely integrated communities at the request and through the generosity of Anglo-Norman lords and of Irish princes alike, and it would be a mistake to confuse an element of chauvinism with narrower and politically motivated Anglophobia. In 1216, as we have seen, the abbots of Mellifont and Jerpoint had had to be replaced, and in 1220 and 1221 the general chapter of the order had indicated continuing concern. The abbot of Clairvaux himself was detailed to attend to Mellifont and her extensive filiation, and in 1227 his deputies, one French and one English, reported the existence of disaffection on a scale to warrant the instant deposition of five of the abbots. It was also decided to break up the whole Mellifont filiation by making major houses such as those at Monasteranenagh and Baltinglass subject not to their mother but to various English houses. It was to implement this policy that the abbot of Clairvaux sent over one of the ablest men in the order.

Stephen of Lexington's arrival in 1228 shaped Irish Cistercianism for the next three centuries. His powers were dictatorial, but his exercise of them far from tyrannical. Hard-core dissidents were transferred to other houses, some of them outside Ireland, and postulants were not to be received who had no French and Latin, a practical exclusion of many Irish vocations though possibly not intended as such. Irish monks were not to be eligible for election to abbot at any of the houses other than Abbeyshrule, Corcomroe and Newry, though it was made clear that the ban would eventually be lifted, and that in the event of a vacancy at these three relatively unimportant houses an Irishman would have to be elected. At Monasteranenagh Stephen encountered armed resistance, with troops having to be brought in, and at Mellifont there was a walk-out by a large proportion of the community. Ultimately, though, the will of the general chapter prevailed, and it was decided to break up the Mellifont filiation, the different houses being affiliated either to Clairvaux itself or to Fountains in Yorkshire, to

Furness in Lancashire, or to Margam in Wales. The prospect of there emerging a distinctively Irish version of Cistercian monasticism seemed to have been shattered for good, but it was not a victory of Anglo-Norman over Gael. Only a century later there were to be Anglo-Irish complaints that houses such as Mellifont and Monasteranenagh were practising discrimination against Englishmen! At the end of the year the death occurred of the archbishop of Dublin, Henry of London, and his successor as metropolitan was an innocent English nominee of Hubert de Burgo's, a certain Luke, surname unknown, who is historically remarkable only for his longevity. He was to occupy this critical see for nearly thirty years, but fails to rate an index entry in any of the standard outline histories of mediaeval Ireland. He was a pastor and not a politician, and his preoccupation with the affairs of his own province goes far to explain why, over the next quarter of a century, there should have emerged a degree of equilibrium where the partitioning of the episcopate between Irish and Anglo-Irish was to be concerned.

Superficially the year 1229 may have seemed uneventful enough, but crucial for the future was the passing by inheritance to John fitz Thomas Fitz Gerald of the great estates in Desmond and across Waterford which had been granted in the first place to Thomas Fitz Anthony. The accession to Shanid of these lands laid the foundation of the future greatness of the Geraldine line of Desmond, and the transfer was both smooth and effective. Not so unspectactular was the reversion to Hugh de Lacy of his old earldom of Ulster which had been authorised in 1227 but which took a considerable period to achieve. Ulster had been in the king's hand, and a further complication was the presence of the Scotto-Norse who had begun to colonise the northeastern littoral. In 1228 the castle at Coleraine was rebuilt, and in general de Lacy does seem to have been able satisfactorily to incorporate the surviving newcomers into his area of influence. At the other end of his lordship, too, he was able to take possession of the important de Verdon lands in Louth which had come to him by marriage but which he had not scrupled to lay waste only a few years before. After 1230, moreover, the Ulster lordship was further strengthened as a result of the death of Aedh O Neill, de Lacy's old ally and neighbour. For a number of years the resurgence of Gaelic Ulster was notably arrested by the flickering up once more of the old feud between the O Neills proper and the remnants of the Mac Loughlins. Also removed by death in 1230 was another veteran of Irish resistance to the invader, Dermot Mac Carthy, and here, of course, the principal beneficiary was the Geraldine house of Shanid.

In the meantime the intruded Aedh O Connor was chafing under the restricted kingship allowed to him by Richard de Burgo, and it is possible that he had had some inkling of future developments in England. However. this may be, he now chose to bid for support from the Irish west of the Shannon by hosting into northeast Connacht. De Burgo's reaction was to throw his weight behind another O Connor contender for the kingship, and his choice fell on one of Aedh's nephews, Felim, a brother of the murdered Aedh. Together they invaded Connacht from the south, and passed by Loughs Corrib and Mask to reach the vicinity of Clew Bay before swinging northeastwards to cross the Curlews near Boyle. Aedh's chief lieutenant was routed, and he himself took refuge in Ulster. Felim assumed the kingship, but within a year proved as intransigent as his uncle, and was imprisoned at Meelick. By 1232, however, Aedh had patched up an accommodation with de Burgo, and the latter had begun to build a castle at Galway, while one of his lieutenants threw up another at Dunamon, west of Roscommon town, to command the strategic crossing of the Suck.

By this time Hubert de Burgo's power and influence in England had reached new heights, and in the summer of 1232 he himself assumed the Irish justiciarship so that his nephew could be deputy and the two salaries accrue to the one family, or possibly to furnish him with a power-base in Ireland in the event of trouble in England. William Marshal, though, had died the previous year, and it seemed that there were none in the English baronage prepared to band together to withstand the de Burgo monopoly of power. Hubert was toppled even so by a coup led by the bishop of Winchester, Peter des Roches, and his Poitevin nephew, and by the end of July Richard's days as justiciar were clearly numbered. On 3 September an emasculated version of the justiciarship was conferred on Maurice fitz Gerald Fitz Gerald, 2nd Baron Offaly, whose mother Eva was a Bermingham heiress, and whose cousin was John fitz Thomas Fitz Gerald of Shanid. From this day we should perhaps talk of Anglo-Irish rather than Anglo-Norman interest in Ireland. The grandchildren of the original conquistadors may still have spoken a certain amount of French, but henceforth the most obvious and also the most convenient division of the inhabitants of Ireland is between the Englishry and the native Irish. Overwhelmingly the rank and file of the colonists, the yeoman farmers and the petty bourgeoisie of the towns, were from England, and the leading-strings which Henry III now sought to impose on Maurice Fitz Gerald betray recognition of the fact that the interests of the colony at large, and not just of the great lords, no longer necessarily coincided with those of the English Crown.

Even before his formal supersession Richard de Burgo had received peremptory orders to reverse his Connacht policies. With respect to the O Connors, he was to set at liberty Felim whom he had arrested the previous year, and by implication abandon Aedh with whom he had been reconciled. While the ex-justiciar haggled with the English king over such issues as the surrender of his castle at Meelick, in the event not insisted upon, the surrender of the royal castles to Peter des Rivaux, the bishop of Winchester's nephew, and the finances of his tenure of the justiciarship, Felim O Connor gathered an Irish hosting and recovered Connacht. The rival Aedh was slain together with a brother and two nephews, and the de Burgo castles at Galway and Dunamon were slighted. It was to be a little time before Henry III's initial delight at this humiliation of de Burgo changed to concern. In May 1233 the English king was still urging Felim to winkle the ex-justiciar out of Meelick where the Irish king had so recently been a prisoner, and in July Henry ordered the restoration to power of a notable Mac Carthy claimant, Cormac Finn, who had likewise fallen out with de Burgo after having been a loyal ally in the expedition to Galway in the previous year. By now, though, Henry III was contemplating a personal inspection of his Irish lordship, but the writing should have been seen to be on the wall where Irish hopes of redress were concerned, when in August arrangements for the royal visit were countermanded as the result of a rebellion in Wales. The leader was Richard Marshal, Earl of Pembroke and Lord of Leinster, who had succeeded his brother William in 1231, and an autumn expedition by the king was a costly failure. Accordingly it was decided to hit at Marshal through Ireland, and by January 1234 instructions were sent to the justiciar and others of the great Anglo-Irish lords to attack his Irish lands. Officially the king was not congnisant of what was afoot, and great play was later made of his signing documents he had not read, but in fact he must have been privy to the designs of his mischievous councillors who were headed by the bishop of Wincester, Peter des Roches, who had pulled down Hubert de Burgo. To overcome the reluctance of the Anglo-Irish lords to round on one of their own number, it was even clearly indicated which of their victim's estates would go to each of the conspirators. When news reached Wales that his Irish lands were under attack, Richard Marshal crossed over in February and mounted an effective counter-offensive. A parley was negotiated, and on 1 April Richard came to the Curragh of Kildare accompanied by a small number of his household and a larger number of his Anglo-Irish tenants. They were outnumbered by the justiciar's company. The talks broke down, and in the affray that followed Richard's tenants abandoned him. The earl himself was carried off a gravely wounded prisoner to his own castle at Kilkenny where on 16 April he died. Ironically a coup in England was even then in process of removing from office Peter des Roches and his Poitevins, and the conspirators now found themselves in a very awkward position. The king officially wept instead of applauding, and on 28 May Gilbert Marshal received all his murdered brother's possessions and honours. Maurice Fitz Gerald as justiciar felt particularly compromised, but in September was persuaded to visit the king, and it was clear that a veil was to be drawn over the whole unhappy affair. On the other hand there were men who had to be paid for the service they had rendered the crown in resisting Richard Marshal's counter-offensive. The lands of Leinster were no longer available, and it was agreed that the answer to the problem was Connacht. Geoffrey de Marisco, too, was a convenient scapegoat, and over the next few years he was to be frozen out of Ireland, outlawed, and ejected from Scotland before dying in exile. Death had already removed another of the less scrupulous of the new generation of colonial opportunists when in 1233 William de Lacy was slain by the O Reillys when raiding into Cavan.

In the meantime the Irish of Connacht and Munster had

been having a field-day. Felim O Connor broke out eastwards into Westmeath and burned the castles at Horseleap and at Mount Temple near Moate. Donagh Cairprech O Brien, de Burgo's old ally, rounded on Limerick and also harried part of southern Galway where the Irish stood by their disgraced master. In Desmond Cormac Finn Mac Carthy struck northwards to Tralee but was heavily defeated by the Anglo-Normans who were apparently led by John fitz Thomas Fitz Gerald of Shanid. Gaelic Ulster was distracted by dissensions between the O Neills and Mac Loughlins, not to mention the old feud of the O Donnells with the territories to the east, and so did not share in the Irish resurgence. By the summer, however, it was clear that the risings had been premature, and they had achieved little beyond affording the government of the colony an excuse for the conquests of the following years. Cormac Finn made his peace with John Fitz Gerald who may not have been anxious for external intervention in the affairs of his corner of the island, but Thomond and Connacht lay wide open. For a consideration of 3,000 marks Richard de Burgo had not merely been restored to Henry III's favour, but he was now being urged to bring his lordship back into subjection, and every encouragement was given to the great Anglo-Irish lords to share in the work and the spoils.

In 1255 Maurice Fitz Gerald as justiciar led the grand attack on Connacht. With him were Richard de Burgo and Hugh de Lacy, and the presence of Ridelisfords, Cogans, Roches, Prendergasts, Berminghams, Butlers and Fitz Griffins either is attested or may be inferred. The host crossed the Shannon at Athlone and arrived at Boyle by way of Roscommon and Elphin. Discipline was lax, but restitution was made by the commanders when the sacristy of Boyle Abbey was looted. Felim declined to be brought to battle, and after reaching

Ardcarne the invaders turned suddenly southwards to deal with Donagh Cairprech O Brien. Felim loyally went to Thomond's support, and it seems to have been in the course of this campaign that he surprised and burnt Meelick. A pitched battle went badly for the allies, and Donagh Cairprech sued for peace and obtained it, but Felim himself took refuge in Donegal, and the colonial host went westwards into Connemara and then up the west coast of Connacht plundering and ravaging as it went. Local collaborators made boats available and the off-shore islands were not immune from this orgy of destruction as the colonists moved through the modern Cos. Mayo and Sligo as far as Ballysadare, with special attention being paid to the lands under O Donnell protection in what is now Co. Leitrim. It was then the turn of the men of north Connacht again, and the island-fortress on Lough Key was forced to surrender after a siege in which catapults, a mole, and even fireships all played their part. Felim, however, judged that the time had come to make his peace, and negotiations with de Burgo resulted in an arrangement whereby he should become the tenant of the five Roscommon cantreds opposite Longford and Carrick-on-Shannon.

In 1236 de Burgo visited England, and in his absence Maurice Fitz Gerald recognised as king of Connacht yet another O Connor claimant, Brian, a second cousin once removed of Felim's. Other cousins of both contestants were involved in a destructive and suicidal war of attrition and recrimination, and Felim ultimately emerged as the strongest single force among the Irish of Connacht. He retained de Burgo's confidence, and inflicted a humiliating reverse on Brian at Rinndown on Lough Ree. Returning from England de Burgo did not openly support him, but he was able to hold his own against the justiciar in the five cantreds while de Burgo in effect held his corner by bringing to heel the O Connors of his lordship proper. By 1237 Felim's position was such that Maurice Fitz Gerald was happy enough to withhold recognition no longer. The rival Brian entered a monastery, and the Anglo-Irish were free to begin parcelling out the enormous lands of their conquest.

For himself de Burgo reserved the plains between the Shannon and Loughs Conn, Mask and Corrib. Hugh de Lacy received five cantreds in Sligo, but leased them to Maurice Fitz Gerald who acquired from the grantees adjacent territories which were neatly rounded off when de Lacy renounced in his favour his claims as earl of Ulster to Fermanagh and Donegal. That the Ulidian colony survived may in fact owe much to this restraint, as there is evidence that the grip of other lords on their existing lordships was seriously weakened when they had to scrape the barrel to find men and resources to exploit the new grants beyond the Shannon. The justiciar also received minor grants in Mayo and the south of Galway, while the west of Sligo went to Piers de Bermingham who had in addition the important barony of Dunmore in the north of Galway. The principal Mayo tenants were Miles Nangle ('Milo de Angulo'), scion of the Costelloes, Jordan of Exeter, Hugh Butler, Adam of Staunton, Gerald Prendergast, and the bastard Cork Geraldine Robert of Carew. Only the last appears to have planted with the thoroughness necessary to secure permanence, and even these descendants of Welsh and Flemish mercenaries ultimately went native. In central Galway the principal tenants were John Cogan and Meiler Prendergast. The *caput* or chief town of the new lordship of Connacht was to be Loughrea, and work was begun on a great castle worthy of an honour or combination of fiefs which on parchment was as great as any in the realm.

The following years were comparatively uneventful as the O Connors who had largely withdrawn into the modern Cos Roscommon and Leitrim licked their wounds, and the various new tenants of de Burgo began the major task of dotting with castles the conquered territory. This spate of castellation is specifically remarked in the Irish annals for 1237, and undoubtedly put a heavy burden on the resources of the newcomers. Little help could be expected from the Crown, and in the very same year the Church was asked for another 'aid' or voluntary tax to help the royal finances at a time of economy if not poverty. In 1238 Maurice Fitz Gerald and Hugh de Lacy addressed themselves to Ulster and threw their weight behind Brian O Neill, Aedh's son, who was enabled thereby to supersede Donal Mac Loughlin. When, however, the primatial see of Armagh fell vacant the following year, the politics alike of English and of native Irish were rendered irrelevant by the papacy's prompt provision to the see of a German, Albert Suerbeer, who was to show himself an admirable defender of Armagh's rights and traditions. It was not until the summer of 1240, though, that the English king accepted the position, and the new primate did not arrive in Ireland until 1241. In the meantime interest continued to centre on Ulster. In 1240 there died Donal Mór O Donnell, the real architect of relative stability in the northwest, and Donegal was exposed to heavy pressure from the Geraldines of Sligo who had parchment title to the whole area. The position was largely redressed, though, when Brian O Neill in alliance with the O Donnells finally smashed the Mac Loughlins in a battle at the unidentified 'Camergi', slaying Donal Mac Loughlin himself and ten of his immediate kindred. Not only was Brian's position in Tyrone now unassailable, but Malachy O Donnell had a claim on his gratitude in the event of Geraldine pressure on the Erne frontier building up to an intolerable level.

In 1241 Walter de Lacy died. He was old and blind,

and his son and grandson alike had predeceased him, so that the heirs to Meath were two grand-daughters. Neither made a spectacular match, and the result was that the great lordship was broken up between two relatively undistinguished houses. The elder heiress married a minor Butler and de Verdon heir, and the younger a French favourite of the king, the respective *caputs* of the new lordships being Ballymore in Westmeath and Trim respectively. Another casualty of 1241 was Gilbert Marshal, Earl of Pembroke and Lord of Leinster. He was childless like his predecessor, but his lands passed smoothly to his brother Walter. The following year saw the death of another figure from the past, Donagh Cairprech O Brien, his successor being his son Conor who had to endure a progressive whittling away of some of the better Thomond lands over the next decade. Henry III by now was becoming bogged down in his continental ambitions, and an expedition to Poitou at the end of 1242 involved a number of Anglo-Irish lords. Among those who died in the campaign were the justiciar's eldest son, Gerald Fitz Gerald, the scion of the barons of Offaly, and Richard de Burgo. Of the latter's three sons Richard only was of age, and when he died in 1248 it was necessary to appoint a custodian, Piers de Bermingham, until Walter should attain his majority. Last of the 'old guard' to die was Hugh de Lacy in 1243, and the Ulster earldom then reverted to the English crown. The grant of 1227 appears in practice to have disinherited his daughter Matilda who married a Geraldine baron of Naas, and for more than a decade the administration of the lordship was entrusted to royal seneschals. The ultimate beneficiary was undoubtedly Brian O Neill beyond the Bann. Intermittent interference even by an energetic justiciar was quite another thing from the constant pressure of an ambitious and expansionist neighbour with local knowledge of the ebb and flow of O Neill internal politics.

In 1244 Henry III was involved in preparations for an expedition to Scotland, and it is interesting to find him summoning to personal service not just the great Anglo-Irish lords, many of them with estates on both sides of the Irish Sea, but native Irish princes. Among them were Brian O Neill and Malachy O Donnell, and it is clear that the English king assumed their obedience even though Ulster west of the Bann in fact still enjoyed virtual autonomy. Those summoned also included Felim O Connor who at the beginning of the year had ventured over to England and made personal complaint at Windsor concerning the fate of the kingdom of Connacht. Henry III had professed concern, but instructions to right the wrongs had been ignored and in fact would never be implemented. Presumably Felim still hoped for much from a projected visit by the English king which had been publicised as early as December 1243, and already there may have been indications of mounting royal dissatisfaction with Maurice Fitz Gerald's justiciarship. In 1245 Felim accompanied Maurice to Wales when the latter brought over some 3,000 men to Deganwy where the king in person was campaigning against David ap Llywelyn. The ill-disciplined reinforcements arrived too late to be useful, and Henry's annoyance was plain. In October John Fitz Geoffrey was chosen as justiciar, and in November the appointment was made public, even though he did not arrive in Ireland until the following summer. His wife was the widow of Walter de Lacy's son and the great-granddaughter of Strongbow, and so there were a few pickings of dower-land to be taken up, but he himself had no formal stake in Ireland. He was indeed the archetypal Englishman sent over to Ireland to govern but very soon became a prisoner of the Anglo-Irish establishment. Maurice Fitz Gerald had the good sense not publicly to resent his supersession, and it was not long before fitz Geoffrey was implementing policies which were in essence those of his predecessor. Two deaths within a fortnight towards the end of 1245 made the position within the colony of Maurice Fitz Gerald even more dominant. They were those of the brothers Walter and Anselm Marshal, the last of Strongbow's grand-sons, and with them the Leinster title became extinct. The great lordship was divided up between the five sisters and their husbands, the new lordships being those of Carlow, Kildare, Kilkenny, Leix and Wexford, and the family names of the ultimate holders Bigod, de Vesci, de Clare, Mortimer and de Valence respectively. We are on the verge of the period when English magnates would be absentee lords of a very substantial proportion of some of the most settled lands of the entire colony.

Among the native Irish relative peace had reigned. Of considerable interest was a dispute within the chapter of Elphin with an appeal to Innocent IV at Lyons before the election of Eoghan O Mugroin as bishop went through in 1245. Henry III recognised the choice, and the episode is a good example of the future pattern of evolution whereby there grew up two parallel Churches, one among the Irish and the other among the English, which coexisted in quite remarkable harmony as long as there was no external interference with the internal affairs of either. Eoghan, however, did not live many months, and in 1246 a new election was necessary with the choice falling on one Tomalty O Connor. The same year Maurice Fitz Gerald invaded Donegal which was officially partitioned between an O Connor puppet, Cormac, a grandson of Rory, and Malachy O Donnell. By November, however, O Donnell was sacking the bailey of the new castle at Sligo where the garrison retorted by hanging the O Donnell hostages from the keep, and in January 1247 the Geraldines mounted a second invasion. Malachy O Donnell was killed while attempting to hold the line of the Erne, and Maurice Fitz Gerald sought to impose a puppet king Rory from the alternative O Connor line. In 1248, however, he in turn was slain by Malachy's brother with the significantly Norse name Gofraid who went on to reassert O Donnell supremacy over Donegal, and so the first Geraldine offensive ground to a halt. Further to the south there had been serious disturbance in Connacht where an O Connor dissident, Turlough, and a roving malcontent from Ossory, Donagh Mac Gilpatrick, headed an insurrection which ravaged from Loughrea westwards, burnt the town and castle of Galway, and inflicted heavy casualties on the feudal hosting sent against them. There was parallel action in Mayo by another O Connor dissident, Tadhg, whose operations ranged from Lough Carra to the vicinity of Castlebar. The Anglo-Irish reaction was to sack Roscommon and Ardcarne, presumably because Felim was held technically responsible for failure to hold in check the native Irish of Connacht. Jordan of Exeter appears to have been the most prominent of the Anglo-Irish commanders, and in 1248 he again headed the forces that ravaged around Westport in retaliation for the burning of Piers Poer's castle. The deaths of leaders such as Tadhg and Dermot O Connor, however, were followed by the collapse of a movement which at one time had seemed likely to threaten the whole colony west of the Shannon.

Also in 1248 Maurice Fitz Gerald attempted intervention in Tyrone where Brian O Neill thought it best to give hostages and so deny the Anglo-Irish a pretext for overt conquest. A bridge was built actoss the Bann at Coleraine and covered by a new castle at Killowen, but the justiciar was in no position to do more than secure the lower Bann against the resurgent power of Tyrone. At Armagh the primate Albert Suerbeer had resigned in 1246, but the papacy once more filled the see by provision, and the new primate was an Italian Dominican, Reginald the Penitentiary, who may even have known St Dominic. Politically his appointment in 1247 was uncontroversial, and he did not take possession of his see until the following year. If it is to the credit of the pope that the primatial see was kept above the political arena, one cannot ignore the fact that the papacy was becoming increasingly interested in Ireland as a source of revenue. In 1245 the justiciar Maurice Fitz Gerald had been warned by the English king not to permit papal emissaries to mulct the Irish clergy as they had the English, and despite this it was alleged that a certain John the Red had persuaded the Irish to part with the very substantial sum of 6,000 marks.

Ireland was still a source of profit to the English crown, but more and more Henry III and his great lords were preoccupied with their own disputes and with various continental adventures. Consistently the justiciar lacked the men and the resources to mount a full-scale assault on the increasingly recalcitrant Irishry, and there was no longer the immigration into Ireland which would have made possible the systematic exploitation of further conquests. It is probably no coincidence that the de Cogan family, which figures among the Connacht grantees a decade earlier, provided a notable casualty back in Desmond in 1248 when Geoffrey de Cogan was slain by Fineen Mac Carthy, a cadet claimant for the succession to Cormac Finn who had died in 1247. He was avenged a year or two later by John fitz Thomas Fitz Gerald of Shanid, a Geraldine who had conspicuously refrained from diverting his resources away from Munster, but it is very noticeable at this period that many of the junior Irish princes were beginning to compete for popular support by dissociating themselves from the collaborationist policies of their seniors. For the time being the crisis in Munster was contained by the refusal of the house of Shanid to be lured away on adventures such as the plantation of Connacht, but the recourse to

the murder of the official Mac Carthy successor, Donal
Got, by John Fitz Gerald in 1252 is evidence of the serious-
ness of the situation. The disaffection was not confined to
Munster. In Leinster in 1249 Fitz Geoffrey devastated
large areas in an attempt to put down an insurrection
headed by 'the sons of kings', and in Connacht the
disturbances were even more serious. The main inspiration appears to have come from Felim's son Aedh who
apparently felt that his family's influence was being
eroded by the policy of collaboration with the Anglo-
Irish of which his father was so conspicuous an exponent.
A daring ambush near Sligo resulted in the death of
Piers Poer and six of his companions, and Aedh proceeded to harry the Anglo-Irish lands between the Moy
and Collooney. Gerald de Bermingham was one of the
victims, but a major loss for Aedh was the death of
one of his ablest lieutenants, his kinsman Donagh. Maurice
Fitz Gerald organised the defence of the colony, and
Felim foresaw that retaliation would fall on the O Connors
generally and so got the bulk of the cattle away to the
north across Breifne. A grand pincer-movement was
then mounted by the Anglo-Irish with Fitz Geoffrey
crossing the Shannon at Athlone, Fitz Gerald advancing
northwards across Galway, and the two armies converg-
ing on Elphin. As usual a dissident O Connor was to
hand, Turlough a nephew of Felim's and he was installed
as king. Breifne was pillaged, and Fitz Geoffrey fell back
into Meath while Fitz Gerald pushed northwest into
Sligo. Felim took refuge in Tyrone, but his son slipped
southwards through the widening gap between the two
Anglo-Irish armies, burned Dunmore and advanced on
Athenry. The Anglo-Irish of southern Connacht concentrated there under Jordan of Exeter, and when battle
seemed likely to be joined sought a week's truce in
honour of the feast of the Nativity of Mary (8 September)
and the Exaltation of the Holy Cross (14 September).

Aedh had been joined by Turlough, presumably because no plausible O Connor could have been with the Anglo-Irish, and Turlough urged an armistice. On 8 September, though, Aedh insisted on fighting, but his troops lost their nerve when so many Anglo-Norman knights debouched from behind the town's flimsy defences, and the rout was complete. Among the Connacht dead lay Donagh Mac Gilpatrick from Ossory, an almost Russell-esque figure who prefigures resistance heroes of our own time. A master of disguise, he had repeatedly penetrated the towns of the Englishry to collect information. Aedh himself escaped, and so did Turlough, but the Anglo-Irish victory was not followed up.

Such passivity, understandable when one recalls how the Anglo-Irish were under pressure to support Henry III in his mounting difficulties at home and abroad, encouraged Felim O Connor to mount in 1250 an offensive which carried him from Tyrone across Cavan and into the O Connor lands of north Roscommon. The colonists' initial response was to blind a number of hostages held at Athlone, but they soon recognised the inevitability of Felim's restoration when they were in no position to put into the field a major army. Turlough O Connor, like so many other tools of the Englishry who had ceased to be useful, was quietly dropped, and Felim further secured his position by expelling from Connacht yet another potential rival, Cathal, who took refuge with the O Reillys. It appears that Maurice Fitz Gerald acquiesced in this arrangement because he refused to be diverted from what he conceived to be the key to the whole problem of the Irishry, the reduction of the North. In 1249 the O Don-nell line in the person of Gofraid had been temporarily ousted from power in Donegal by Maurice's creature Niall O Cannon, and with his left flank covered Maurice now hosted northeastwards to Tullahogue. His advance and withdrawal were harried, but he failed to bring

Brian O Neill to battle, and the campaign's sole outcome was the restoration of O Donnell supremacy. The luckless Niall O Cannon had provided an obvious scapegoat, and had been seized treacherously only to be killed while attempting to escape. The truth was that the Sligo line of the Geraldines lacked the resources to make war on neighbouring Irish princes with any prospect of enduring success. Henry III was increasingly looking to Ireland for revenue and aid, and this was well illustrated when Conor O Brien was confirmed in his kingdom of Thomond on payment of 2,200 marks. Although, too, the English king was able to persuade Pope Innocent IV to condemn Irish attempts to prevent *de iure* election of Englishmen to Irish sees, the *de facto* position obtained that certain sees were thought of as 'English' and others as 'Irish'. In this very year, for example, the distinguished scholar Florentius ('Flann') Mac Flynn seems to have had no difficulty in succeeding Marianus ('Maelmhuire') O Loughnane as metropolitan of Tuam. The very next year, too, there met at Tuam a major synod of the Irish Church, though unfortunately we are given no indication of the scope of its deliberations.

In the late 1240s there occurred a major reform of the English coinage, and at the end of 1251 a new 'Irish' coinage was put out by the newly reconstituted mint at Dublin. An English clerk in the king's service, Richard of Haverhill, had the general oversight, and there is reason to think that the more immediate execution of the work was let out to two Londoners on a commission basis. Before the mint closed early in 1254, a total a little in excess of £40,000 had been struck. The distinctive obverse design was retained, but the new reverse was identical with that of the new English coins, and they were struck to exactly the same weight and fineness. Only pennies were issued, and once again the great majority of them were shipped over to England to assist the royal finances. Exchanges were opened at Limerick and Carling-ford, and all payments to the crown after a given date would have had to be made in the new money at face value or if in the old at a very heavy discount. That there were no branch-mints is evidence not only of the tightness of royal control on an operation that was devised essentially as a source of profit to the crown, but also of how precarious was the English hold on large areas of the country. Many of the new pennies found their way in due course to the Continent, and within a decade they were the subject of skilful imitation in Flanders and in Westphalia. Again, too, it is clear that the issue came to an end because of a drying up of the source of silver, obsolete coin rather than newly mined bullion. While, then, Henry III's government was busying itself with what it could get out of Ireland, the local administration was attempting to complete a conquest which it knew only too well was no more than nominal where vast areas of the island were concerned. The bridling of Ulster re-mained the prime objective, and in 1252 Maurice Fitz Gerald rebuilt the castle at Cail Uisce (Narrow Water) on Lough Erne to menace Tyrone from the southwest, while in Down another castle was built at Mag Coba often identified as Dromore but perhaps closer to the Mournes. A subsequent hosting was something of a fiasco, and the Meath and Munster contingents came to blows in Dundalk with the Munstermen suffering numerous fatalities. The threat to Gaelic Ulster was unmistakable, and in 1253 Brian O Neill followed up a very successful repulse of a hosting by Maurice Fitz Gerald from the southwest with an irruption into the plain of Down which not merely slighted Mag Coba but devastated a number of centres of Anglo-Irish settlement. There was no day of reckoning. Henry III urgently needed his military tenants for service in France, and the glee of the native Irish as great lords such as Fitz Geoffrey and especially Maurice Fitz Gerald crossed the Irish Sea, was reported to the English king and remarked by him. He had always recognised the desirability of a more personal acquaintance with Irish affairs, but in 1233 and again in 1243 projected visitations of the lordship had been shelved. Now at the beginning of 1254 there was to be a return to the thinking of his grandfather, the devolution of the lordship on a son, but with a difference. This time the new lord of Ireland was not a little boy lacking an inheritance but the heir to the English throne, the pubescent Edward who already was being groomed for the succession.

6 Resurgence and Equilibrium

THE state of Ireland in 1254 was one of uneasy balance with the advantage and to some extent the initiative still inclining to the Englishry. In Ulster the ambition of Brian O Neill represented perhaps the most overt threat to the colony, but a flaw in his position was his inability to bring to heel Gofraid O Donnell whose position in what is now Donegal proved unassailable. Further to the south the colonists seemed firmly entrenched in North Connacht, though the rivalry of Walter de Burgo in the west and of Maurice Fitz Gerald with more than a foothold in the hinterland of Sligo, was to prevent serious exploitation of the position. As regards the land corridor over to Leinster, the Irish position was perhaps no more seriously weakened by the rivalries of the O Rourkes and the O Reillys than was the English by the loosening of the old de Lacy hold on what is now Westmeath as a consequence of absentee de Verdon lordship. In South Connacht there was already manifest what was for Ireland a quite unusual father-and-son partnership in the persons of the shrewd Felim O Connor and the dynamic Aedh, while a virtual lacuna in our sources for Thomond cannot quite conceal the burgeoning of something comparable, where Conor O Brien and the still youthful Tadhg were concerned. In Desmond the position was confused but already it was obvious that in the person of Fineen Mac Carthy Munster would have a champion efficiently ruthless as regards his Irish as his Anglo-

Norman neighbours. It would be many a long day before the colonists again would have arrayed against them so much talent and enterprise, yet Prince Edward's thoughts seemed all of Gascony and of the war in France. For several years, too, Henry III was to retain in his own hands enough power in respect of Ireland for it to be not altogether surprising that his son found his new lordship insufficiently challenging to engage his personal intervention. Again and again there was to be talk of a visit by the lord himself, and again and again Irish hopes of redress – and Anglo-Irish fears – were to be excited and allowed to cool.

In 1255 Aedh O Connor made a dramatic journey to the North. He brought back from Tyrone the political refugees from Connacht whose presence at the court of Brian O Neill represented a very real threat to the security of the line of Cathal Crobderg. Brian in fact was renouncing any idea he might once have had of imposing his power on his most powerful neighbour to the south, and an attempt to define his more limited sphere of influence with greater precision by a campaign against the O Reillys proved abortive. In the meantime Felim O Connor was strengthening his position by entering into direct negotiation with Henry III, and he was also able to come to some sort of understanding with Walter de Burgo. It is unlikely to be a coincidence that the native Irish Archbishop of Tuam, Flann Mac Flynn, was himself negotiating with Henry III, and in fact died at Bristol in the course of a second visit the following year.

It could well have been the *rapprochement* of the King of Connacht and the English King that induced Walter de Burgo to attempt a decisive weakening of his old adversary before Henry III's favour could become effective. Allying himself with the O Reillys he failed to make the necessary rendezvous, and the O Connors were able to inflict a heavy defeat on his

Irish allies at Mag Slecht in north-west Cavan. The O Reillys were then left to the tender mercies of the O Rourkes who obtained a notable victory at Farnaght in what is now Co. Leitrim, while for his part Walter de Burgo was sidetracked into an eventful but largely inconsequential attack on the O Flahertys in Connemara. Felim showed a much more statesmanlike appreciation of the realities of the situation by coming to Rinndown where he parleyed with Alan la Zouche, Edward's newly appointed justiciar replacing his steward Richard de la Rochelle who had been acting intermittently in this capacity. Alan gave an undertaking that Felim's lands were not in jeopardy, and the King of Connacht went on to Athleague where he had talks with the returned John de Verdon concerning the sensitive lands along the Shannon where both had interests. That an accommodation was reached is suggested by the fact that it was at this juncture that the O Rourkes fell out with Felim – any resumption of de Verdon power in this area directly menaced Breifne. The Irish continued to fight among themselves until the following year, but Henry III was preoccupied with France and with a resurgence of Welsh nationalism, and if Brian O Neill was holding his hand others of the Irish of Ulster were preparing to enter the field. Maurice Fitz Gerald was dead and Gofraid O Donnell struck south across the Erne to slight Narrow Water, obtain a signal victory at Credran, and burn Sligo, while in Ulidia one of the last Mac Dunleavy dynasts attacked the colonists with considerable success. The shadow if not the substance of these events probably explains why it was that Felim was able to restore his essential position at a parley at Athlone at which both Alan la Zouche and Walter de Burgo were present. At the end of the day Felim could look back on 1257 with some satisfaction. The most serious reverse perhaps had been Henry III's intrusion of Walter de Salerno into the metropolitan see of Tuam, but the interloper was to prove short-lived – and a notable absentee into the bargain.

During 1258 the initiative seems generally to have been with the Irish. In Desmond, for example, Fineen Mac Carthy was busily consolidating his position, while in Connacht the colony lost a very experienced local administrator when the sheriff Jordan of Exeter was killed by Hebridean pirates who had taken a rich prize off Connemara. Interestingly the sheriff had had at his disposal naval forces comparable to those of his adversaries. The political event of the year, however, was a meeting at Narrow Water on Lough Erne of the Connacht and Thomond heirs-apparent, Aedh O Connor and Tadhg O Brien, with Brian O Neill. Brian, unabashed by a reverse near Letterkenny when trying to overcome the dying Gofraid O Donnell, seems to have received some sort of recognition as the leader of the new Irish resurgence, but Aedh obtained the very solid advantage conferred by O Neill recognition of O Connor overlordship of Breifne. Subsequently he was able to intervene in the dynastic troubles of the O Rourkes, and it is perhaps indicative of *de facto* O Connor autonomy that Felim was conspicuous by his absence when an overall peace was concluded between the Anglo-Irish and the native Irish generally. The prime benefactor on this occasion appears to have been Conor O Brien who had been engaged in heavy fighting with the English of South Connacht to retain his lands in the south-west of what is now Co. Galway, but once again Felim could look back on the year with a sense of achievement. Not the least of his coups had been the translation of his kinsman Tomalty from Elphin to the archbishopric of Tuam, and as an added precaution the new metropolitan had been packed off to Rome to receive the pallium. Since 1255 Cashel had been occupied by the formidable

David Mac Carvill, and at this very moment another Irishman, Abraham O Connellan, was establishing himself at Armagh. Only at Dublin was an Englishman an Irish archbishop, Fulk of Sandford papally provided in 1256, and he was to show himself by no means subservient to secular interests. It was perhaps in an attempt to instil a new urgency into the direction of the affairs of the colony that we find Alan la Zouche being replaced as justiciar at this juncture by Stephen Longespée, a bastard cousin of the king's. The new administration showed itself, though, little if at all more forceful, and the only event of 1259 to bring comfort to the Englishry was the premature death of Tadhg O Brien. Ominous for the future was the marriage at Derry of Aedh O Connor with a daughter of Dougal Mac Sorley, Lord of the Isles. With the bride as dowry came 160 Scotto-Norse mercenaries, the gallowglasses who were to revolutionise warfare in Ireland by their capacity to withstand the onset of the Anglo-Norman knight. The bridegroom also took advantage of his journey northwards to rendezvous yet again with Brian O Neill, this time at Devenish on Lough Erne. The Ulster pot was coming to the boil.

In 1260 Brian O Neill, supported by Aedh O Connor but by neither the O Donnells nor the O Briens, launched a major offensive against the English colony in Ulster. Strategically the project was ill-conceived, just as diplomatically it was a disaster. His target should have been the justiciar's feudal host which was in no shape to take the offensive, and the time was more than ripe for a statesman to cash in on increasing Anglo-Irish resentment of government by 'English by birth'. Stephen Longespée if not already ailing or even dead had exhibited no particular competence, and Brian's intervention in Ulidia should have been in the guise of a suave liberator. Instead he appeared as a swashbuckling Gaelic crusader, and the colonists were offered the simple alternatives of withstanding him or of being driven into the sea. Commendably they stood their ground, and on the ridge of Drumderg just outside Downpatrick, the Irish host was locked in battle with the English levies on 14 May. The latter were better armed and with superior fire-power seem to have had little difficulty in beating back repeated charges by the unmailed and impetuous Irish. The flower of the Gaels of Ulster fell, Brian among them, and if Aedh himself escaped, the Connacht casualties were only less severe. The battle was decisive for the shape of Ulster down the centuries, and perhaps for the shape of Ireland as well. It was small comfort for the Irish of Munster that Conor O Brien was able to inflict a severe check on the young Maurice Fitz Gerald at Feakle in what is now Co. Clare, while as ever Fineen Mac Carthy maintained his pressure on the increasingly embattled Anglo-Irish of Desmond. The Irish position in Ulster was gravely weakened. Among the O Neills there was a disputed succession with Aedh Buidhe initially and with English favour displacing the young Donal; while to the west the spirited Donal Óg O Donnell, with gallowglass support derived from his Mac Sweeny marriage, was building up a Gaelic dynasty in what is now Donegal which for two and a half centuries would exhibit consistent hostility to its O Neill neighbours. Truly Brian O Neill has much to answer for inasmuch as the most bitter element in an admittedly ancient rivalry had been his cynical if abortive attack on the mortally wounded victor of Credran in 1258.

The discomfiture of Aedh O Connor could not but be followed by a recrudescence of de Burgo power in Connacht, but for the time being it was confined to an invasion of what is now Roscommon. The O Connors wisely fell back to their natural fastnesses, and a peace was concluded. A similar attack on Donegal by Maurice Fitz Gerald more positively miscarried after an initial success, and the following year saw remarkably little serious fighting where Connacht was concerned. Generally the O Rourkes were able to slacken the O Connor hold on Breifne, while John de Verdon, now finally returned from France, was quietly consolidating his position east of the Shannon by the erection of a castle at Moydow in what is now Co. Longford. The great event of 1261, however, belongs to the extreme south-west of the island. In the spring Fineen Mac Carthy mounted a whirlwind campaign against the remaining Anglo-Norman castles in what is now south Kerry and west Cork, and his unbroken success seriously alarmed the Shanid Geraldines who invoked the assistance of the new justiciar William of Dean, a stop-gap until Prince Edward and Henry III should name ʼa successor for Stephen Longespée. William had had considerable Irish experience, and brought south substantial reinforcements. His strategy seems to have been to cut Desmond in two by slicing across the base of the Beare peninsula. Fineen, however, somehow lured the Anglo-Normans up the funnel of the valley of the Slaheny tributary of the Roughty just south of Kilgarvan, and on 24 July at a point near Callan the flagging knights were rushed by the Desmond ambushers. The slaughter among the Anglo-Irish was immense. Eight barons and twenty-five knights were the most distinguished of the victims, and they included John Fitz Gerald and his son Maurice. The surviving heir of the house of Shanid was an infant in his cradle. William of Dean is heard of no more. Had he died of wounds – or of chagrin? His successor was once again Edward's steward, Richard de la Rochelle. It was no time to entrust Ireland to a newcomer. Nor is it surprising that the English king accepted the succession at Armagh of the Irish Dominican Mael Patraic O Scannell.

In the event the colony weathered the crisis. Fineen Mac Carthy took the offensive again, but was killed with many of his captains in an attack upon Ringrone Castle near Kinsale. With their backs to the wall the Anglo-Irish of Desmond fought well, and it was the story of Drumderg all over again. Fineen's successor was an able brother Cormac, but the weakness of the Irish of Ulster meant that the O Connors in particular were exposed to reprisal, and in 1261 came retribution. In May Henry III had summoned to England Richard de la Rochelle, Walter de Burgo, Maurice Fitz Gerald and others. It may be supposed that the riot act was read on the dangers of dissension, and on their return to Ireland two major campaigns were mounted against the Irish of Connacht and Desmond. The first was to take the form of a pincer attack with de Burgo coming in from the west and the justiciar and de Verdon from the east. The O Connors however, slipped through the trap, and their willingness to ravage their own lands meant that there was little booty to comfort the invaders. The site for a castle was marked out at Roscommon, but Aedh O Connor timed his overtures to coincide with de Burgo's wearying of the struggle, and it was not long before a peace was concluded. Heavy fines were inflicted on the O Connors, but payment was more or less easily evaded, and Aedh could be well satisfied with the outcome. De Burgo then proceeded to Munster, while the others turned back into what is now Longford and Westmeath with the intention of clipping the wings of the renascent O Farrells. Both expeditions failed to live up to expectation. Gilla na Naomh O Farrell survived all attempts to depose him, and Walter de Burgo and Cormac Mac Carthy fought a drawn battle at Mangerton near Killarney, though the death in action of Cormac undoubtedly proved a heavy blow to Irish morale.

In 1263 it seemed for a time that there would be foreign intervention in Ireland such as had not been seen for a century and a half. The reports of the Scotto-Norse mercenaries in the service of the O Connors and the O Donnells may well have excited the ambitions of Haakon IV of Norway who had been brought to Scottish waters by a dispute over the Isles, and certain of the Irish promised supplies and winter-quarters if he would intervene against the English. The bait was tempting, but before a decision could be made Haakon had been worsted by the Scots at Largs and his death followed shortly afterwards. It was perhaps to stiffen resistance in the north-east that a few months earlier Walter de Burgo had been granted the revived earldom of Ulster to hold with Connacht, and a nominal exchange of relatively minor lands in Tipperary still left him easily the most powerful single lord in Ireland. In England, however, Henry III's relations with his baronage were deteriorating rapidly, and with his father John's example before him the cultivation of the Anglo-Irish was an obvious policy. Certainly when the crunch came the magnates at least in the colony were for the most part staunchly royalist. De Verdon happened to be in England at the time of the battle of Lewes (14 May 1264) and shared the king's captivity, and it would seem that Maurice Fitz Gerald was motivated more by personal resentment against the favoured de Burgo than by positive sympathy for de Montfort when, on 6 December 1264, he clapped into prison Richard de la Rochelle and two other notables. It afforded de Burgo, of course, no less satisfaction to take reprisals against the too vulnerable Geraldine lands in north and south Connacht, and the prisoners' captivity lasted only until April. The truth was that confusion reigned. In mid-June 1264 what may have been the first of the new-fangled parliaments on the English model had been held at Castledermot. It was essentially an amplification of the council with the principal officers of state joined by those great lords without whose co-operation the colony could not have been well governed. In place of the captive Richard de la Rochelle, Geoffrey de Joinville acted as justiciar with the consent of the majority of the Anglo-Irish, and de Montfort vainly besought Archbishop Fulk of Sandford to take over in the interests of peace. The colony in fact seems to have been well aware of the danger of disunion, and minor Irish depredations in Westmeath and in Sligo were a running reminder of what could happen if the troubles in England were allowed to spill over into Ireland. On 15 April, de Joinville obtained from a representative assembly of the greater lords a critical guarantee that land-titles obtaining in 1264 would be respected, and the escape of Prince Edward in May and the release of Henry III after de Montfort's overthrow at Evesham (4 August) had few repercussions in an Ireland that had ignored attempts to find alternatives to de la Rochelle and de Joinville (*i.e.* Roger Waspail on 6 May and the ambitious Bishop of Meath, Hugh of Taghmon, on 10 June). Another factor in the colony's weathering of the storm was the death of Felim O Connor. Inevitably Aedh was preoccupied for a time with securing his succession, and it is perhaps significant that in 1266 his inaugural attack upon the English was confined to the Geraldine lands in Offaly. De Burgo, he rightly felt, would be slow to take up arms on behalf of Maurice Fitz Gerald, and de Burgo was far and away the most formidable of the Anglo-Irish.

In 1267, however, Aedh was seriously ill – the rumour was that he was dead – and he had not been able to prevent the English of Connacht from making serious depredations on lands that traditionally had looked to the O Connors for protection. In 1268, too, the native Irish suffered a further setback when Conor O Brien was murdered by a cousin. The balance was restored and more, though, when Aedh O Connor inveigled a major expedition sent against him into the woods to the west of Athlone and inflicted a considerable defeat. It is a measure perhaps of the inability of the colony's administration to prosecute a strong policy of conquest that in Desmond the O Driscolls were merrily disputing the Mac Carthy ascendancy by sea as well as land. The naval battle was reputed one of the most hard-fought ever to have occurred in Irish waters. The English justiciar, David de Barry, clearly lacked drive, but his successor, Robert of Ufford, was to demonstrate the dangers of precipitate militancy. Profiting from a recurrence of Aedh O Connor's illness, he began anew work on the castle at Roscommon, and his example was followed at Sligo by Maurice Fitz Gerald. The O Donnells, however, retorted by burning Sligo in 1270, and on his recovery Aedh O Connor took up the new challenge from Walter de Burgo. The latter invoked Ufford's assistance, and the colonial army pursued Aedh on a wild-goose chase through the bogs and scrubland of what is now Leitrim. There is no evidence that Aedh threw in his gallowglasses, but when the Anglo-Irish knights flagged they were overrun by the Connachtmen at Athankip near Carrick-on-Shannon. Their rout was complete, and the numerous fallen included Walter de Burgo's brother, William Óg, executed after the battle as a reprisal for Walter's slaying of Turlough Ballach, an O Brien princeling, who had accompanied the Connacht army. Ufford, of course, was discredited, and Walter de Burgo was never the same man again. From Thomond came news of a further reverse when Brian Ruadh O Brien took Clare Castle, but if Aedh O Connor was able to slight or burn half-a-dozen Anglo-Norman castles and towns he was not able to protect his own in Sligo, and it is clear that individual marcher lords were able to contain the Irish resurgence in the absence of concerted action by the native Irish. The slayings of O Reilly and O Farrell princes suggest that a rising east of the Shannon was abortive, while in Desmond there continued the civil war among the Mac

Carthys too characteristic of the history of this century. Ulster seems to have remained generally quiet, but one interesting development was the unusually prompt election of Nicolas Mac Aleese to succeed O Scannell in the see of Armagh, and ultimately the appointment received the approval of the English king. Both at Armagh and at Cashel Irish interests were to be well served for the rest of the century, and it is worth recalling that in 1269 David Mac Carvill had become a Cistercian. In 1272 he founded an abbey at Cashel, and in 1274 largely unpicked Stephen of Lexington's work by restoring to Mellifont her filiation. The colonists insinuated anti-English sentiment, but it was this same archbishop who later was to throw his whole weight behind the appeal to the English king for common law to be extended to the native Irish.

On the first anniversary of Athankip, Walter de Burgo died at Galway. His heir was a young boy, and so his lands in Connacht and in Ulster passed into the custody of the English crown. That the death of their old adversary did not provoke an immediate reaction among the native Irish may reflect the fact that it was a year of bad weather and of famine. The new English justiciar, too, James of Audeley, was showing himself both efficient and energetic, and the absence of a strong O Neill was another incentive for the Irish chieftains of Ulster to put themselves under the protection of the King by making their submissions. In Connacht, on the other hand, Aedh O Connor was at the height of his reputation, and in 1272 he slighted Roscommon. Audeley, who had campaigned with success against the resurgent Mac Murroughs and O Byrnes in what is now Carlow and Wicklow, moved to meet the menace, but died as a result of a fall from his horse. In this crisis one of the 'English by birth', Maurice Fitz Gerald, was appointed justiciar, but Aedh crossed the Shannon and ravaged as far as Granard before turning back and breaking the bridge of Athlone. Later his fleet was master of Lough Ree. He failed, however, to follow up these victories, and in 1273 the only major campaign was an expedition by Maurice Fitz Gerald to Thomond which effectively overawed O Brien and outflanked Aedh. Wicklow, on Dublin's doorstep, continued to give trouble, and in the protracted absence of Edward I, who had succeeded his father in 1272 but was lingering on the continent, Geoffrey de Joinville was named justiciar. His first campaign in Wicklow in 1274 was undistinguished, but in Connacht the death in May of Aedh O Connor transformed the whole situation. The O Connors threw up three kings before the year was out, and it was only after a long period of internecine war that Tadhg O Connor, a distant cousin of Aedh, received some sort of general if ephemeral recognition. In the meantime de Joinville had restored the castle at Roscommon. In Wicklow, however, success continued to evade the justiciar, and in 1275 he was sharply defeated at Glenmalure. Ulster, too, was restless, and in 1276 there was heavy fighting. A complicating factor here was the feuding between the Anglo-Irish of north Antrim, the famous quarrel of the Mandevilles with William fitz Warin, the royal seneschal.

It was at this juncture that demands from the Irish to be accorded common law rights reached a new crescendo. That there was opposition from the Anglo-Irish was not surprising. The opportunities for exploiting the native Irish would be severely circumscribed if the victims could sue in the royal courts before judges who might well be 'English by birth'. That Edward I did not insist on the concession is less understandable. He was consistently seeking to bring Ireland into conformity with English practice, and his replies to repeated episcopal complaints concerning infringements of traditional rights labour this point even when some of the most persistent of the petitioners were impeccable in their English descent and allegiance. However, Edward's first preoccupation was always with his wars in France, Wales and Scotland, and he seems to have hesitated to bring about a head-on collision with the Anglo-Irish lords. In the event, though, many of the better-off native Irish living among the Englishry were able to purchase the required standing, and the sums raised were timely even if it was putting on the long finger a problem that would haunt Ireland for centuries. In the event, too, one wonders whether the English king would not have done better in purely financial terms if he had accepted the 1276 Irish offer of 8,000 marks – more than £5,000 – for a grant to the Irishry at large. If 1277 saw a victory by Ufford at Glenmalure, it also saw further antagonisation of the more responsible of the Irish when the collaborationist Brian Ruadh O Brien was summarily hanged at Bunratty by Thomas de Clare as a scapegoat for a failure involving heavy Anglo-Irish losses. Further to the north, Tadhg O Connor had entered into an alliance with Donal Óg O Donnell, and the provocative castle at Roscommon was once more slighted. The following year, however, Tadhg was murdered, and the able and energetic Ufford virtually expropriated the whole of the south of what is now Co. Roscommon. In Thomond the O Briens continued to fight among themselves with Thomas de Clare very much enjoying the role of *tertius gaudens,* and a sharp reverse for the Anglo-Normans at Quin proved only a temporary setback. In 1279 Irish hopes of a general grant of English law were finally dashed to the ground, and the death of Tomalty O Connor ushered in for the metropolitan see of Tuam a *sede vacante* status which was to last for almost a decade. It is, though, a measure not of blatant English intervention but of Irish acceptance of the fact of increasing English control over large areas of Ireland that the reign of Edward I is marked by an appreciable fall in the proportion of Irishmen occupying Irish bishoprics. Dublin, too, had shown Edward how profitable a metropolitan vacancy could be for the Crown which claimed the revenues of all sees in the limbo of an episcopal interregnum – it was only in this very year that John of Darlington, a Dominican fiscal expert, had become Archbishop of Dublin in succession to Fulk of Sandford who had died in 1271! To add to the scandal there is no positive evidence that John ever set foot in his archdiocese!

In 1280 the young Richard de Burgo nicknamed the 'Red Earl' was deemed of age. Friction between the O Neills and the O Donnells seemed to guarantee his Ulster lands a measure of security, and in Connacht the emergence of Cathal Ruadh O Connor as an acceptable king probably promised more of stability than menace. Only in distant Desmond was there overt Irish resurgence in the person of Donal Óg Mac Carthy. In 1281 the great O Donnell leader, Donal Óg, invaded the heartland of O Neill power, but he was killed and his forces utterly routed, in a disastrous battle fought at Desertcreagh near Dungannon. The Anglo-Irish under Thomas de Clare dominated Thomond from their new castles at Bunratty and Quin, and it was a measure of Irish demoralisation that Donal Óg Mac Carthy was able to mediate between the rival O Brien cousins, Donagh and Turlough, while in north Connacht there was a sensational affray within the Englishry between the Cusacks and the Barrats. In November of the same year Ufford was superseded as justiciar by another of Edward's ecclesiastical financiers, Stephen of Fulbourne, Bishop of Waterford. The new stability in the colony had meant that the recoinage of 1279 in England could be extended to Ireland, and even Roscommon was contemplated as an exchange if not a mint. As it was, Dublin from 1280 and Waterford from 1281 converted perhaps £50,000 of old coin into new pennies, the great majority of which found their way across the Irish Sea, and relatively few halfpence and farthings were left to meet local requirements. That Waterford was chosen for the site of the second mint doubtless reflects Stephen's eye for his own interests – he was to acquire a reputation for peculation to which the king was induced to turn a blind eye only by his unrivalled efficiency. By 1283 both mints had closed, apparently because supplies of bullion had been exhausted, but they had served their purpose. On the political front there seemed little to report. In 1282 Murtagh Mac Murrough had been killed in battle with the Crown forces deployed southeast of Dublin. In the following year internecine war among the Ulster Irish had resulted in the death of Aedh Buidhe O Neill at the hands of the MacMahons and the O Reillys of Breifne to the profit of his second cousin Donal, the son of the Brian killed at Drumderg. In 1284 there were raids by the English of Connacht against the native Irish, but Cathal Ruadh O Connor redressed the balance by a slighting of Kilcolman. In the same year dissension among the O Briens in Thomond was largely resolved by Turlough's slaying of Donagh, though for the moment the position of Thomas de Clare must have seemed unassailable. In 1285 the Cusacks received a bloody nose at the hands of Magnus O Connor, Cathal's brother, but in a battle in the Ox Mountains the victors were routed by Philip Costello, while further south Thomas de Clare had little joy when campaigning against the largely reunited O Briens. Only in 1286 was there a flicker of the old hostings of the past. Richard de Burgo brought together a major army and swept across Connacht and Ulster where Niall O Neill was installed ephemerally in place of Donal, but in retrospect the triumph was largely empty. The death of Maurice Fitz Gerald the same year and of Thomas de Clare in 1287 removed significant bulwarks of the old order. Quin was slighted in 1287, and the O Connors seemed to enter on a new phase of resurgence when in 1288 Magnus deposed his brother. Richard de Burgo attempted to intervene, but found that the Geraldine interest and others among the Anglo-Irish were by no means prepared to see Connacht pass entirely under his control. When, too, Stephen of Fulbourne died the same summer, the justiciarship remained firmly with the 'English by birth', his successor being John of Sandford, another tried and trusted servant of the Crown who since 1285 had been Archbishop of Dublin. Stephen, incidentally, had been elevated to the metropolitan see of Tuam in 1286, but interestingly his place at Waterford had been taken by his brother Walter, his deputy as Treasurer between 1281 and 1283. What Edward wanted in Ireland was unspectacular but solid progress to stable government. The events of the next few years reveal most of the obstacles that had to be overcome before Ireland could become an integral part of his wider ambitions.

In 1288 there had been a minor insurrection among the Irish of Offaly and Laois, and within days of his appointment Sandford took the field with an energy and competence which deserves its unusually full record in the administrative accounts that have chanced to survive. In the course of the summer he had traversed much of Connacht and Munster as well as Leinster, and he campaigned only less vigorously and extensively throughout the winter. Significantly Magnus O Connor ranged himself on the side of the justiciar, and no less significantly Richard de Burgo was to punish the Irish slayers of the hero of Irish resistance east of the Shannon, Cairpre O Melaghlin. Interest now shifts to Ulster. In 1290 Donal O Neill was able to expel Niall Culanach, while Turlough O Donnell with the backing of his Mac Donnell mother's gallowglasses deposed his stepbrother Aedh. These palace revolutions were not to Richard de Burgo's liking, and the supersession of Sandford as justiciar by a returned

Leinster absentee, William de Vesci, may have seemed to promise a less meticulous scrutiny of two great subjects. In 1291 de Burgo deposed Donal O Neill, but the restored Niall Culanach was promptly assassinated, and Donal's exile only obtained by the substitution of yet another cousin, Brian, who had enjoyed like his father consistent Mandeville support. De Burgo went on to devastate what is now Donegal, and Connacht was quick to offer its submission, though the earl was unable to effect the deposition of Magnus O Connor whose feigned submission the following year he had to accept with the best grace he could. There was a new star in the ascendant among the Anglo-Irish magnates. The Connacht lands of Maurice Fitz Gerald had passed to his nephew John fitz Thomas who in 1287 had added the Geraldine estates in Offaly to his own Sligo inheritance. When Magnus died in 1293, de Vesci interfered to secure the succession of a new Aedh O Connor, and John indicated his displeasure at his neighbour's trespass on his preserves by seizing the unfortunate Aedh. De Vesci obtained his release, but when he tried to take the matter further the king personally intervened to prevent the justiciar attacking the Geraldine patrimony. John fitz Thomas denounced de Vesci to the English parliament, and de Vesci, who seems to have enjoyed de Burgo's backing, next tried to proceed against Fitz Gerald in the council at Dublin. A wordy *cause célèbre* ended in July 1294 when the disgraced de Vesci appeared at Westminster to do battle, while his Geraldine opponent with the support of Peter of Bermingham remained in Ireland in contumacious defiance of the royal summons and coolly proceeded to attack Aedh. The new justiciar, William of Doddingsele, was unable to make any effective intervention, and in December the Geraldines paid off an old score by laying hands on Richard de Burgo's own person. Only in March 1295 was the Earl of Ulster released from captivity, and then at the price of public affirmation of Fitz Gerald's title to all his Connacht lands. The humiliation doubtless explains why it was possible for Donal O Neill to make a new comeback. Brian O Neill was slain in a great battle at Crech Tulcha near Glenavy by Lough Neagh, and his followers were induced to take themselves off and to settle among the Englishry east of the Bann where they constituted the henceforth quite distinct O Neill sept that gives its name to the modern Clandeboye ('clann na Aeda Buidhe'). The battle was a rebuff for de Burgo which would rankle down the years, but more important still the whole incident would colour Donal's attitudes to the earldom of Ulster in the crisis that lay ahead.

Doddingsele had died within months of his appointment, and in Dublin the council had appointed one of the 'English by blood' to act as justiciar until a royal nominee should become available. Their choice fell on another of the Geraldines, Thomas Fitz Gerald of the Shanid line. It was an interesting appointment. Thomas, nicknamed the 'Ape', undoubtedly commanded the English king's confidence – in 1292 he had been granted Desmond and Decies, and by the exercise of model restraint had come to terms with the Mac Carthy of the day, Donal Ruadh, who was allowed to preserve his patrimony virtually intact in return for a nominal rent. On the other hand, he was a Geraldine, and so could mediate on behalf of the contumacious John fitz Thomas of Offaly. He seems to have seen very clearly that Edward I, increasingly embroiled in his wars with France and Scotland, was more interested in reconciliation than recrimination. What the English king wanted from Ireland was the sinews of war, feudal levies, provisions and coin. Thomas' policy, then, was to allow tempers to cool, and his public concern was with the troubles in north Leinster where he was successful in obtaining the submission of Maurice Mac Murrough a new thorn in the side of the Dublin authorities. Since the previous year an attempt had been made to resume the striking of coin despite the fact that supplies of bullion just were not available. Under Thomas Fitz Gerald the Dublin mint remained open, but the Waterford establishment was moved to Cork. The Fulbourne precedent suggests that there may have been personal advantage in this transfer, and it is very noticeable that under the next justiciar coining took place only at Dublin.

In the late autumn of 1295 Edward's choice of a successor to Doddingsele had become known, and by Christmas the new justiciar had crossed over the Irish Seas to take up his office. He was John Wogan, 'English by birth' and a very experienced administrator though apparently without Irish service. His policies were to be directed to two by no means inconsistent let alone incompatible ends. On the one hand, the whole government of the colony was to be made to approximate to the king's English ideal, and Wogan showed himself unusually zealous in securing every regalian right within his power. On the other, Ireland was to be harnessed to the English war effort. Wogan was perhaps not unfortunate in the dearth of constitutional talent which might have opposed some at least of his claims. John of Sandford, for example, who had shown himself a resolute defender of the archiepiscopal privileges of Dublin had died in 1294, and this critical see was now held – one cannot well say occupied – by another Dominican absentee, William of Hotham. He was to be followed by the equally elusive Richard of Feering (d. 1306) and even more shadowy Richard of Havering who resigned before his consecration in favour of the shortlived John de Leake (d. 1313). Among the magnates only Thomas Fitz Gerald could be said to rank as an elder statesman – and he was still not forty and would die in 1298. His kinsman John fitz Thomas was under a cloud, as was

was Richard de Burgo, while in 1297 the disgraced de Vesci would be removed by death. Typical of many minorities was that obtaining in the critical marchland of Thomond where Gilbert de Clare was still in his teens, and events were to show that there were few old heads on young shoulders. Energetic Wogan undoubtedly was, but one may perhaps wonder whether his successes – and he had his failures – did not owe more to consistency and competence than to any particular genius.

Edward had called on Ireland to contribute 10,000 men to the English armies. Technically the island was always under a feudal obligation to furnish rather more than 400 knights, but it would have been unrealistic to expect more than a proportion of these heavy cavalrymen to be available for service beyond the Irish Sea. What Ireland could send, though, was a multitude of light-armed skirmishers, horse and foot alike, who were admirably adapted to the type of campaign on which the English found themselves engaged in Wales and Scotland. By the end of 1296 Wogan was beginning to deliver the goods. A useful and balanced contingent had been dispatched to Scotland, and it included the justiciar himself, Richard de Burgo, John Fitz Gerald, Theobald Butler and others of the nobility. It is no coincidence that in November of that year John Fitz Gerald was pardoned his transgressions against the Crown. It was the king's intention that he should work his passage. Before his departure, too, Wogan had shown himself able to cope decisively with a purely Irish crisis. In Connacht the highly personal rule of Aedh O Connor had resulted in his deposition by his own council in favour of one Conor Ruadh. Aedh, however, had the backing of the local Englishry, and in particular of William de Burgo, Richard's cousin, to whom the 'Red Earl' was entrusting more and more of his Connacht interests. It was, then, with Anglo-Irish contingents at his back that Aedh brought Conor Ruadh to battle, the usurper was slain and a particularly bloody vengeance wreaked on the Irishry most conspicuous in his support. With Wogan as justiciar, however, that was the end of the matter. A few years earlier the de Burgo and Geraldine interests could well have been at each others' throats.

The year 1297 was one of shortages and mortality. There was continuing trouble with the Irish of north Leinster, and Leighlin was burnt. The strained relations between the Anglo-Irish and the Native Irish – the latter perhaps too openly exulting in their newfound respectability as valued soldiers of the English king – were well seen in a affray in Dundalk which resulted in the deaths of a number of Richard de Burgo's O Hanlon and Mac Mahon 'satellites' – Irish skirmishers – returning from services with their lord. Edward was anxious that a major contingent should serve in France, but only John Fitz Gerald appears to have gone. However, his was a special case in that some of his unresolved difficulties with de Burgo made it particularly desirable that he should not fall again from grace. Wogan for his part was applying himself with his accustomed assiduity to administrative reform, and Meath and Kildare which had come into the king's hand were constituted counties. To obtain a platform for his policies he now convened at Dublin what is often considered the first Irish 'representative' parliament. The single chamber was composed of the higher clergy and greater lords together with two nominees from each of nine counties and five liberties together with the sheriffs of the same. The spirit of the assembly was ominous, and reflected an embattled colony. Irish manners, dress and speech were belittled, and the term 'degenerate English' first applied to those of the colonists who had tried to adapt themselves to Irish ways. Other whipping-boys included absentee landlords, magnates who recruited Irish henchmen, and those men of property unwilling to share in the defence of the colony. This negative outlook is one that was to be depressingly characteristic of Anglo-Irish imitations of the English parliament right down the centuries.

The year 1298 was relatively uneventful. An expedition to Thomond was necessary to raise the siege of Bunratty where Turlough O Brien had bottled up Gilbert de Clare, but a more significant development was the first manifestation of a willingness on the part of John Fitz Gerald to relinquish the controversial lands in north Connacht. By the following year the Geraldine presence in Sligo was a thing of the past, and de Burgo's lands in theory swept in an unbroken crescent from the Atlantic to the Irish Sea. In 1299, too, there was a further development in the constitution of the embryonic parliament when the towns but not the shires and liberties were summoned to a parliament. In 1300, on the other hand, when taxation figured on the agenda both the 'popular' interests were summoned, but Wogan soon found it more satisfactory to try to negotiate finance with individual towns and counties on a piecemeal basis. He was moving almost continually around the colony, and in the north the reformed de Burgo – in 1299 he had even been appointed deputy justiciar for a few months – was applying himself no less sedulously to the consolidation of his great lordship. By 1300 the whole of the coastal plain of North Derry appears to have been under his control, and in this year he began to establish himself in Inishowen. The parallel construction of a major castle at Ballymote to cover the approaches to Sligo was an only less obvious threat to the O Neills, and a well-founded fear of encirclement as a preliminary to destruction goes far to explain Donal's behaviour over the next two decades. Among the Irish the gallowglass had become a costly fact of life, and it is no coincidence that Irish annals had recorded in 1299 the death of Alexander Mac Donnell,

Lord of the Isles and something of an enterpreneur where this particular commodity was concerned.

In 1301 Wogan took another army over to Scotland, and de Burgo on this occasion chose to remain at home without apparently forfeiting the royal favour. Wogan, on the other hand, was to receive at least an implied reproof for undue zeal when he had eventually to restore to Joan de Valence her inheritance in Wexford which he had taken into the king's hand just a little too precipitately. There was need to avoid treading too obviously on Anglo-Irish toes when so much of the island remained to be pacified. In 1302 there was fighting in what is now Carlow, Wicklow and Wexford, and the death of the statesmanlike Donal Mac Carthy promised a fresh period of instability in Desmond. In July of that year the death of Stephen O Bracken could have exposed the metropolitan see of Cashel to interference, but in the event the vacancy was filled by another moderate Irishman, Maurice Mac Carvill, so that the death in 1303 of Nicolas Mac Aleese of Armagh could be regarded from an Irish point of view with equanimity. Other events of this year included another hosting to Scotland in which de Burgo participated – he now had a Scots son-in-law as a consequence of the marriage of his daughter Elizabeth to the widowed magnate Robert Bruce. More than twenty years after her marriage she was to bear him a son who would make the 'Red Earl' grandfather of a king, but in 1302 all this lay very much in the future. In 1304 de Burgo suffered heavy domestic loss with the deaths one after the other of his wife and eldest son, but in 1305 we find him building a major castle on the western shore of Lough Foyle at the modern Greencastle. Further south Wogan's hands were full with war in Leinster where the seneschal of Wexford fell in battle, and also in Desmond. Pacification was not made easier by Irish resentment of Anglo-Irish contempt for the native Irish which at this juncture plumbed new depths when Peter of Berming-ham's castle at Carbury was the scene of a cynical and treacherous massacre of more than thirty of his Irish neighbours, the victims allegedly including his infant godson dashed to the ground from the battlements of the lofty keep. In 1306, though, Bermingham experienced some retribution when his forces were smartly defeated by the Irish of Meath, and Wogan himself took the field yet again in Wicklow. In Connacht there was open dissension between Aedh O Connor and a very sub-stantial proportion of his subjects led by Aedh Brefnech of another line, while the death of Turlough O Brien in Thomond exposed the Irish of that area to new attacks from a Gilbert de Clare ever anxious to exploit a disputed succession. In the north an Anglo-Irishman, John Taafe, was finally consecrated to Armagh, but he was dead within months and it is doubtful if he ever as much as saw his cathedral. It is significant that in this same year Mellifont forfeited its temporalities or fiscal privileges for ignoring a royal command of 1297 that half of the com-munity should be Anglo-Irish or English. More momen-tous was the news from Scotland. Robert Bruce had had himself proclaimed king towards the end of March. By the winter Edward's armies, which still included major contingents from Ireland, had driven him from Scotland, and it was supposed that he lurked on Rathlin with the tacit connivance of his father-in-law Richard de Burgo whose daughter Elizabeth languished in captivity in England. In 1307 he returned to Scotland, and his success stung to fury the aged Edward I who died in July while personally directing the campaign which it was hoped would settle the Scottish problem once and for all.

Even in more felicitous times Edward's death would have had repercussions in Ireland, and Wogan was attempting to govern an island which had been bled white by demands from the English king for supplies for his Scottish wars. The Irish were insurgent in the midlands where Geashill was burnt and the Englishry of Roscommon routed not by the O Connors but by one Donagh O Kelly, a reminder of the fact that other Connacht families were assuming a new importance. The O Connors were racked and weakened by internecine strife of which the latest manifestation was the slaying by Aedh Brefnech of one Donal, the other Aedh's designated successor and one who might perhaps have reunited the people at large behind him. In England it was already becoming only too clear that Edward II was of very different stuff from his father, and Wogan's task was becoming fast impossible. The year 1308 began badly, and south of Newcastle West a cousin of the dead Thomas the 'Ape', Thomas fitz John Fitz Gerald, was killed and the castle at Killeedy burnt by two very minor Irish princes acting in concert, Conor O Brien and Cormac Mac Carthy. This was an area not previously disturbed, and a punitive expedition into Desmond largely failed although supported by a contingent of the O Briens who were still hopelessly divided between themselves. It was only a crumb of comfort that Conor O Brien was wounded when joining in another Mac Carthy attack on Kilbolaine Castle near Dromcolliher which miscarried.

Wogan for his part was not inactive. A positive achievement was to mediate between the principal O Brien contenders, a Donagh and a Dermot, if only because one ugly new development was the circumstance that both enjoyed Anglo-Irish backing, Donagh being supported by William de Burgo and Dermot by Richard de Clare who succeeded his childless brother Gilbert this same year. Limerick was thus relieved of its invidious position between the contestants. In north Leinster, however, things went less well, and the Irish burnt Athy. In the early summer Wogan took the field in person, but his troops were severely mauled in Glenmalure. Before the position could be restored the politics of England once more impinged directly on the Irish scene. Edward II's magnates had banded themselves together to secure the downfall of Piers Gaveston, the king's hated favourite, and the pill was sugared by the parliament's dispatching him to Ireland as the king's lieutenant. On literally the previous day Richard de Burgo had been named Wogan's successor, but now for nearly a year the government of the colony was in the hands of a fallen courtier entirely without experience of Irish affairs. The wonder was that more damage was not done, while in Wicklow indeed Gaveston showed more than competence, rebuilding castles and driving a military road to Glendaloch. When he returned to England, however, Wogan resumed the justiciarship and had to address himself less selectively to the problems of the island as a whole.

In at least two areas the colonists were warring among themselves. In Wexford the Condons and Roches were at each others' throats, and in Meath, with Richard de Burgo's backing, Walter and Hugh de Lacy of Rathwire were disputing by force of arms the feudal descent of certain lands, and had bottled up Theobald de Verdon in the castle at Athlone. The native Irish could not well chortle. Soon Aedh O Connor was to fall at the hands of his old rival Aedh Brefnech, and in the following year Desmond as well as Connacht was thrown into confusion with the deposition of Donagh Mac Carthy in favour of Dermot Ruadh. In the February a royal official John Boneville had been slain by the Wicklow Irish, allegedly with the connivance of Arnold le Poer, and in the same month the best contribution that a parliament convened at Kilkenny could make to the crisis was to enact that *nullus merus hibernicus*, on the face of it 'no mere Irishman', should be admitted to any religious house or benefice in the colony. To his credit the English Dominican Walter Jorz, Archbishop of Armagh since 1307, intervened with

Edward II to have this new specimen of Anglo-Irish malice immediately annulled, and it is interesting that some of the magnates made similar representations. Already within the colony there was emerging a divergence of interest between the great and the bourgeois, and one of the weaknesses of the Anglo-Irish parliament was that too often it afforded a platform for the purblind pettiness of small-minded men without real responsibility for the conduct of affairs. In Connacht things had gone from bad to worse. Aedh Brefnech O Connor was assassinated by his own captain of mercenaries, significantly a Mandeville, and for nearly a year William de Burgo ruled Connacht virtually as an O Connor king. The Mac Dermotts were the focus of Irish opposition, and threw their weight behind Felim O Connor of the rival line who was ultimately accepted by de Burgo but opposed by Rory a brother of the dead Aedh Brefnech. It was perhaps as much to prejudice this rival's case as to fan Gaelic sentiment that Mulrooney Mac Dermott had his godson Felim brought to Carnfree and there inaugurated as the O Connor with every last detail of traditional ceremonial and ritual that bard and brehon could recall or devise.

In 1311 there was again notable feuding between the Anglo-Irish of Wexford, and it was the same story among the Irishry of Desmond and of Thomond. The rivalry of the O Brien claimants extended to their supporters, and the position was further complicated by the intervention on opposite sides of Richard de Clare and of William de Burgo. During the fighting de Burgo was taken prisoner and only released after giving an undertaking to abstain from further interference in Thomond. In the meantime Donagh O Brien had been murdered, and Dermot had been recognised by most of the Irish of Thomond. Unabashed de Burgo threw himself behind a new candidate, the dead Donagh's brother Murtagh, and a solution to the problem of the O Brien succession seemed as far off as ever. In Wicklow the O Byrnes and O Tooles continued to be a thorn in the side of the Dublin government, and the burning of Saggart not ten miles from the capital demanded action. The position was restored by one of the 'English by blood' Edmund Butler who took command of a major expedition which penetrated Glenmalure and brought the O Byrnes temporarily to heel. In November Walter Jorz resigned the see of Armagh in favour of his brother Roland, another Dominican, who was to hold the primacy for a decade before himself resigning. We do well to remember, however, that Termonfeckin and not Armagh was the normal seat of Irish primates who were not of Irish blood, though events were soon to show that ecclesiastical appointments still were not always political. At Tuam in January 1312 William of Bermingham died after a pontificate of nearly a quarter of a century – he had succeeded Stephen of Fulbourne – and consecrated in his place was an Irishman, Malachy Mac Hugh. In Thomond Dermot O Brien was preoccupied with revolts among his own subjects, and in Meath and Louth the new pretensions of the revived de Lacy line alarmed the cadet de Verdons to such an extent that they took the law into their own hands. Wogan marched to Drogheda, while a detachment of his army pushed ahead to Ardee. The uninvolved Anglo-Irish were appalled by the prospect of the royal army waging war on the 'English by blood', and Wogan was persuaded to leave the restoration of order to the local magnates. Before the advance party at Ardee could be pulled back, however, it was attacked by the cadet de Verdons on the pretext that it had been laying waste the countryside, and heavily defeated. Before the position could be redressed, a frustrated Wogan had laid down his justiciarship, and in the absence of an appointment by the otherwise preoccupied Edward II the council in Dublin appointed Edmund Butler fresh from his success at Glenmalure.

The focus of interest now shifts again to Munster. In 1313 Dermot O Brien died, and Murtagh Mac Turlough once more invaded Thomond. The new de Clare protégé was one Donagh O Brien, and with the support of most of the Irish of Thomond he was able to push Murtagh and his followers back over the Connacht border. When, though, Richard de Clare after patching up an accommodation paid a visit to England for the purpose of conducting some family business, Murtagh promptly took the field with the overt backing not only of William de Burgo but also of Thomas Butler, the brother of the acting justiciar. Surprisingly Donagh rallied his forces, and once again Murtagh withdrew into Connacht. Now, however, a purely local vendetta was overtaken by events the other side of the Irish Sea. Edward II had resumed the war with Robert Bruce, and on 24 June 1314 the English feudal host had suffered a disastrous defeat at Bannockburn near Stirling. There was no formal Anglo-Irish contingent at the battle but the death of de Clare Earl of Gloucester could not but have repercussions for the lordship of Kilkenny and for the de Clare interest in Thomond. For some years England had lost absolute command of the Irish Sea, and Robert Bruce feared that when England girded herself for a full-scale war in Scotland, Ireland would be found to have enormous strategic significance as a base and magazine. The Scots did not and could not hope to have the degree of absolute thalassocracy which could prevent English armies in Strathclyde being provisioned and reinforced by blockade-runners from bases and transit-camps in Ulidia only a few hours' sail from Galloway, and so the bulk of the English navy could be concentrated in the North Sea to convoy troops and supplies into the Forth. A further consideration was the need for the

Scottish king to find an outlet for the ambitions and energies of his brother Edward. In the security of victory many in Scotland would be scrutinising very closely the claims and policies of the new monarchy, and Edward Bruce, one of the heroes of Bannockburn, could become a rallying-point for opposition. Dissidents in Ulster, and notably the Bissets with their hereditary feud with the Mandevilles, and Donal O Neill with his personal hatred of Richard de Burgo, could be relied on to harp on the advantages to Scotland of carrying the war over into Ireland, while the mission of John of Hotham in August 1314 was doubtless construed by Robert Bruce as evidence that Edward II's intentions coincided with his own fears. In fact the veteran envoy appears to have been conveying representations from the English king concerning the state of England where there was increasing aristocratic resentment of the royal favourites. Only days before Bannockburn, too, there had been another change in the Irish administration when the council in Dublin had replaced Edmund Butler by Theobald de Verdon, lord of Westmeath, and Edward for his part would be anxious to have up-to-date intelligence of the Anglo-Irish political scene.

Edward Bruce landed at Olderfleet near Larne on 25 May 1315. He brought with him 6,000 men, most of them infantry with long experience of the Scottish wars. The Mandevilles were easily defeated, and Donal O Neill and a few of the Irish of Ulster rallied to his banner. Carrickfergus was invested, and the Scottish army pushed south to Dundalk which was burned (29 June), Ardee and Louth. Opposition to the Scottish invasion centred on two men, Edmund Butler who had been appointed justiciar only in March, and Richard de Burgo who was in Connacht. By the end of July they had assembled major armies and effected a junction of their forces south of Ardee. De Burgo was accompanied by a large native

Irish contingent under Felim O Connor, and persuaded
Butler that his troops alone would be more than sufficient
to deal with the Scots, and that Ulster was his responsibility. He was probably anxious to spare his lordship the
depredations of troops not under his direct control, and
the Scots certainly appeared to have over-extended
themselves. Butler turned back, and de Burgo marched
rapidly northwards. The Scots retreated through Armagh,
and the two armies then lost contact. It would seem
that Edward Bruce fell back across what is now Tyrone,
while de Burgo advanced up the east shore of Lough
Neagh and in his anxiety to winkle Bruce out of his
newly conquered lands in Inishowen and North Derry,
did not trouble to mop up the forces investing Carrickfergus. The two armies next confronted each other at
Coleraine where the bridge had been broken down, but
both were hit by a shortage of supplies. De Burgo was
perhaps not altogether unhappy to have to allow Felim
to return to Connacht where his old rival Rory, who
likewise was in communication with Bruce, had carried
all before him, and the Anglo-Norman host fell back on
Antrim where it could be more easily provisioned. When,
however, the Scots crossed into Twescart, de Burgo
marched north-east to cover Carrickfergus and on 10
September was overwhelmingly defeated at Connor.
William de Burgo was among the prisoners, but Richard
escaped. Many survivors made for Carrickfergus, but
the 'Red Earl' got away with others through the Moyry
Pass. The siege of Carrickfergus was resumed in earnest,
but by mid-November Edward Bruce was again marching
south. This time he was opposed principally by the
returned absentee Lord of Trim, Roger Mortimer,
whose taking up of his lordship in 1308 had been one of
the grievances of the de Lacys. The Scots again passed
through Dundalk and then swung inland to Nobber
before defeating Mortimer near Kells (6 December).

Trim could not be taken, but Edward Bruce was looking for easy victories and turned away west to Granard and Newcastle near Abbeyshrule before spending Christmas at Ballymore. Before the New Year he was on the march once more, and his advance took in Edenderry, Kildare, Castledermot and Athy where he was brought to battle (26 January) at Ardscull by superior forces assembled by Edmund Butler the justiciar, John Fitz Gerald, and Arnold le Poer. Their advantage was thrown away by the divided command, and Edward Bruce slipped away westwards as far as Geashill. Soon after the middle of February, however, his forces had shot their bolt, and it was a hungry and defeated army that fell back through Meath into Ulster. Its morale was not improved when Edward Bruce threw everything into an assault on Carrickfergus, and was smartly repulsed.

Undoubtedly the Scottish army had succeeded in its prime purpose of preventing Ireland being an effective base for an attack upon Scotland. Considerable damage had been done to the colony's economy, and the effects of this had been intensified by coincident famine. Before castles resolutely held, however, he had conspicuously failed, and remarkably few of the Anglo-Irish had rallied to him. This was not altogether surprising when he was seen to court for short-term advantage the native Irish who were soon disillusioned by his open contempt for their interests. Only a week after Ardscull a group of leading Anglo-Irish magnates was coming together to proclaim their loyalty to Edward II, and their profession dated 4 February 1316 bears the seals of the heads of both lines of the Geraldines, of de Clare, of two le Poers and two Roches, and of Maurice of Rochford. In Connacht they saw Edward Bruce associated primarily with the activities of Rory O Connor whose avowed aim was the expulsion of the Englishry, and it was with difficulty that Richard de Burgo and Felim O Connor were keeping their heads above water. Yet the tide was fast turning, and on 16 February 1316 Felim with the support of Richard de Bermingham overthrew Rory near Ballymoe. The breathing-space was sufficient. By the time that Bruce had seduced Felim from his Anglo-Irish alliance, William de Burgo foolishly released from captivity was back in Connacht. On 10 August there was a pitched battle outside Athenry between the native Irish of the West and the Anglo-Irish led by de Burgo and Richard de Bermingham. The Anglo-Irish prevailed, and Irish casualities were so colossal that Connacht was effectively knocked out of the war. There were other consequences. In the north-west the eclipse of the O Connors guaranteed an extension to the power of the O Donnells – the year before Aedh O Donnell had slighted Sligo and taken Carbury under his protection – and in Thomond Donagh O Brien's position was to be seriously undermined by the fact that his old rival Murtagh had been one of the few Irish to be on the winning side at Athenry.

In the meantime Edward Bruce had achieved little of substance. Most of the Irish chieftains of Ulster had rallied to him after his victory at Connor, and on 1 May he accepted from Donal O Neill the kingship of Ireland at an impressive ceremony just outside Dundalk. The de Burgo keep at Greencastle in Inishowen fell, but the capture of the strategically far more significant royal stronghold at the other Greencastle on Carlingford Lough proved a hollow victory when it was soon recaptured by a minor expedition from Dublin. The Anglo-Irish of Leinster and Munster, too, were left undisturbed while they damped down the general but completely unco-ordinated insurrection of the Irish which Bruce should have been directing to a common end. That they failed to succour Carrickfergus is a reproach not to them but to Edward II who alone had the naval resources to break the blockade, but when the castle fell in September the starving garrison was able to negotiate for terms. Even at this juncture a major campaign in the south could have achieved much, but Edward Bruce appears to have lost the initiative. The truth was, of course, that Donal O Neill had led him into an impossible position. As a Scottish general he was committed to a war of devastation which would have spared Irish or Anglo-Irish only to the extent that he might contemplate harnessing either interest to this objective. As 'King of Ireland' he should have had as his first aim the welfare of his new subjects, and by tradition and temperament he was closer to the Anglo-Irish than to those who had crowned him. He fell thus between two stools, and inconsistency was only to be expected when a never very thoughtful man essayed incompatible ends. In England, though, Edward II's hold on the reins of government still did not slacken sufficiently long enough for a coalition of real ability to exploit the colony's new found advantage. In May John Fitz Gerald had been created Earl of Kildare to balance the earldom of Carrick conferred on Edmund Butler in the dark days after Connor, but he died in September only a few weeks after the demise of another senior magnate, Theobald de Verdon. Richard de Burgo, expelled from Ulster and overshadowed in Connacht, clearly had forfeited the public confidence of his fellow-magnates and the English king alike, though his loyalty and military ability were not in doubt. It is not surprising, therefore, that Roger Mortimer's star was in the ascendant, and a timely visit to England resulted in his extra-ordinary appointment late in November as King's Lieutenant. A mission was sent to the Pope to procure the excommunication of Bruce's supporters, but a more practical intervention in matters ecclesiastical would be the nomination to the crucial sees of Dublin and Cashel of two outstanding administrators, Alexander of Bicknor and William fitz John, the one 'English by birth' and the other 'English by blood'. It says much that a weak English king could make dispositions such as these in an island nominally Edward Bruce's, and patently the essential structure of the English colony had not been dismembered by a military presence which seemed as intermittent as remote.

Robert Bruce appears to have had his own suspicions that all was not well, and in December 1316 came to Carrickfergus with a substantial number of fresh troops. It was rumoured that he contemplated a leap-frog extension of the war into Wales, but if so Edward persuaded him to attempt one more throw in Ireland. Winter campaigns favoured the Scottish infantry, and on 16 February the royal brothers crossed the Boyne at Slane. Edmund Butler was absent, and Mortimer not yet arrived. Richard de Burgo, though, was at his estate at Ratoath, and took command of the Anglo-Irish forces. A hastily improvised ambush miscarried, but not until after fighting as hard as any seen in Ireland, and the 'Red Earl' took refuge in Dublin. The Scottish forces which had by-passed the walled city of Drogheda were at Castleknock on 23 February, and the Bruces may have hoped that their discredited in-law would at last side with them, or that the Dubliners would be overawed. In the event the mayor of Dublin had taken it on himself to clap the Earl of Ulster into prison, and the citizens themselves fired one of the suburbs to strengthen the defences. The Scots had no siege-train, and by the next day they had fallen back to Leixlip. By mid-March they were deep into Ossory having arrived at Callan by way of Castledermot and Gowran, with religious houses not exempt from their systematic spoliation. The main Anglo-Irish forces were mustering at Kilkenny, but the Bruces broke away to the west to Cashel and Nenagh. They apparently hoped for much from Donagh O Brien who had been expelled from Thomond and who had abandoned his traditional de Clare alliance in disgust at the favour shown Murtagh by William de Burgo and the Englishry of Connacht. Early in April the Scots were within miles of Limerick, but their advance was now being marked by Edmund Butler and a sizeable feudal army. By the middle of the month the news had percolated that Roger Mortimer had landed at Youghal on 7 April, and was marching north with ample forces to be in at the kill. Butler in fact was holding his hand on instruction from his new superior, and Robert Bruce was shrewd enough to know when the game was up. The Scots slipped quietly away to the east, and by early May they were back in Ulster after a series of forced marches that had taken them back over most of the line of their original advance. Their own devastations of a few weeks earlier meant that they had to endure considerable privation, and it was only when they reached Trim that they were allowed to halt for a week to recuperate. Later Robert Bruce took ship back to Scotland, but for Edward disengagement was not so facile. His Irish kingship was a commitment that could not be severed without humiliation.

Mortimer in the meantime had arrived in Dublin where he obtained the release of Richard de Burgo. He then proceeded to Trim, and the recalcitrant de Lacys were driven into exile. A smart campaign against the O Farrells secured Meath, and he then turned back to bring to heel the Irish of Wicklow. Most of the winter was spent traversing Munster, and by March he was back at Drogheda. It was from a position of strength that Mortimer had ratified the succession in Connacht of Turlough O Connor, Felim's brother, and there was a measure of rebuke for William de Burgo who was later to throw his weight behind a Cathal of the alternative line. For practical purposes the ratification entailed an abandonment of Roscommon, but Mortimer's instructions of

1317 had specifically enjoined the admission of the Irish to English law, and the events of May 1318 were to show the dangers of an inadequately supported presence west of the Shannon. Murtagh O Brien's purely temporary alliance with Richard de Clare had not really outlasted his brother Dermot's slaying of Donagh in a battle at Corcomroe in the late summer of 1317, and de Clare tried to reserve his position by maintaining a possible alternative O Brien in the person of one Mahon who curiously enough had fought beside Murtagh on the Anglo-Irish side at Athenry. This would have made him a more dangerous rival, and for Murtagh there was the further grievance that the upstart should be residing in the old O Brien royal residence at Inchiquin. Murtagh moved against Mahon, and Richard de Clare was forced to intervene. On or about 10 May 1311 the Anglo-Irish force was ambushed at Dysert O'Dea and cut to pieces. Richard himself fell with four of his principal knights, and the few survivors were hunted back to the gates of Bunratty. The castle itself was not abandoned, but there was a frantic evacuation of all but the actual garrison, and for practical purposes the de Clare ascendancy in Thomond had come to an end. Richard's infant son Thomas died in 1321, and the divided inheritance would not attract an adventurer with the initiative and resources to revive old ambitions.

Robert Bruce's departure from Ireland on 22 May 1317 had left the Irish of Ulster entirely dependent for protection on his brother. Robert himself was probably only too aware of Edward's limitations, and it is likely that it was the King of Scotland who suggested – just as it may have been Bernard of Linton, Abbot of Arbroath, who drafted – an appeal to the Avignon Papacy. Donal O Neill undoubtedly stood to lose most from the military débâcle that he may well have begun to foresee, and he seems to have spent much of 1317 canvassing the other

Irish princes for their support. As with the Bruce invasion there was a certain ambiguity of intent, and the document as eventually transmitted through cardinal legates in England to mediate between the kings undoubtedly suffers thereby. One aim was to justify the Irish rejection of Edward II in favour of Edward Bruce by a catalogue of all the enormities that Ireland had had to suffer as a consequence of English misrule. For Robert this would have been the *Remonstrance's* principal function, but it is doubtful if Pope John XXII was open to be persuaded to acquiesce in a *fait* that was not even *accompli*. He was after all Edward II's lord where Ireland was concerned, and the Irish were presuming to impose on him their own choice of successor. The second aim of the *Remonstrance* was more subtle. By the same rehearsal of Irish grievances, and especially of those concerning Anglo-Irish discrimination, Donal and his co-signatories certainly hoped to obtain some protection from future abuse. Nor were these hopes entirely in vain. Pope John was sufficiently impressed to forward a copy of the *Remonstrance* to the English king in the spring of 1318 with a suitable exhortation that any wrongs be righted. If he was in no position to insist that the English king took positive action, the bland assurances of the English king that the grievances were without substance do not necessarily mean that the *Remonstrance* was entirely without effect. Englishmen were beginning to be not altogether happy about the colonial attitudes of the 'English by blood', if only because their tyrannies could provoke situations where trouble and expense would be caused the English government, and Mortimer's 1317 policy of conciliation with special emphasis on grants of English law was continued under the administrations which followed. By the middle of the fourteenth century virtually every Irishman had access to the royal courts who wanted it, but paradoxically it was Irish law that was becoming attractive to one section of the Anglo-Irish. When the cadet de Verdons challenged Wogan in 1312 they were presaging a trend which a quarter of a century later would make Burkes out of many of the house of de Burgo.

In the spring of 1318 the situation in Ireland was such that Edward II felt able to summon Mortimer over to England. The Dublin council, too, must have felt that there was little likelihood of a major new offensive on the part of Edward Bruce's Scots, and for three months a churchman, William fitz John of Cashel, was acting justiciar – Edmund Butler had already vacated the position. In the summer another of Edward II's ecclesiastical appointments, Alexander de Bicknor of Dublin, was named justiciar, and the administration of the colony seemed back at last on a civilian basis, though there was always the precedent of John of Sandford as a reminder that a cleric was not necessarily disqualified from nor incapable of decisive military action. Edward Bruce, however, was still able to take the field, and it was probably to obtain the advantage of surprise that he advanced the date of his winter campaign to the autumn instead of waiting for midwinter. Again he came over the Moyry Pass, but some word of his movements had been received and he was opposed before Dundalk by John de Bermingham with a heterogenous array of regular troops and local levies. It seems that the Scots and their Irish allies together outnumbered the colonists, but that the former on their own were outnumbered but not outclassed by Bermingham's muster. Edward Bruce was urged by some of his officers to pull back and await reinforcements, but he stood his ground and on 14 October it was the English who attacked up the slopes of Faughart. Edward Bruce was cut down by a worthy citizen of Dundalk who himself collapsed mortally wounded over the dead king's body, and the battle became a rout, though the Irish were scarcely engaged and retreated in good order. The survivors among the Scots had barely reached Carrick-fergus and taken ship for Scotland before a fleet under John of Athy was complete master of Irish waters, and the Bruce invasion was at an end. The king's head was struck off and sent to Edward II, and Bermingham created Earl of Louth for his services.

Ireland had known an alternative alien monarchy, and it had proved not at all to her taste. Edward Bruce not merely died unkeened by those whom he professed that he had come to liberate, but the news of his death was greeted with a relief amounting almost to delight. He had been a violent and an impetuous man, and it is significant that his only recorded approximation to a parliament was described in the contemporary record as a hanging one. His raids into the lands of the Englishry had been ruthless at a time of general shortage, and no attempt appears to have been made to save the crops for the starving Irish. To play one class off against another was beyond him, and if there was a complaint among the Englishry that the friars tended to foster Irish dreams of independence, he did not hold back his men from sacking the Franciscan house at Castledermot. Nor does he appear to have been unduly disturbed by the remarkable declaration of one Anglo-Irish friar that the killing of an Irishman was no sin and certainly would not interfere with his saying Mass. There is no doubt that his invasion had weakened the colony, but the relative position of the native Irish certainly had not been enhanced. The economic damage to Leinster was nicely balanced by the carnage of Athenry, and there is much to be said for the view that already under Edward I there has been achieved in Ireland a rough-and-ready equilibrium between the two great interests within Ireland. Each had lost the capacity to render the other a mortal blow, and if the colony seems more impressively monolithic as a result of royal insistence on an English-style administration, the traditional diversity of Irish society conferred a resilience and resistance to change which were truly remarkable. Timely but increasingly occasional genuflections to the power of the moment would enable an Irish king, prince or chieftain to arrive at some sort of *modus vivendi* with his Anglo-Irish neighbours. In this connection it is surely noteworthy that Donal O Neill weathered an attempt to depose him which seems to have been inspired principally by his Clandeboy rivals, and would die in his bed still King of Ulster. It was to be the same story at the other end of the island where Murtagh O Brien would rule Thomond for a whole quarter of a century after his annihilation of de Clare's army at Dysert O'Dea. Nor is it irrelevant that in both these cases the kings would be succeeded in typically Gaelic fashion by a distant cousin from the alternative line.

Bibliography

Outline Narratives

THERE are three major histories which embrace the whole Anglo-Norman period. Oldest but still indispensable is G. H. Orpen, *Ireland under the Normans 1169-1333* 4 vols (Oxford 1911-20: reprinted 1968), which can be said to have shaped a whole generation of subsequent research. Less ponderous perhaps is E. Curtis, *A History of Medieval Ireland from 1086 to 1513* (London 1938: reprinted 1968), a seminal but very readable review of the whole mediaeval period which incorporates more original research than might be supposed, and which is particularly valuable for its lively and sympathetic acquaintance with the Irish evidence. Both the above works, however, need now to be studied in conjunction with A. J. Otway-Ruthven, *A History of Medieval Ireland* (London 1968), the vintage of a life of scrupulous study of the Anglo-Irish archives and likely to be for many years to come the definitive account of the colony's organisation and history. These three histories may profitably be supplemented by J. F. Lydon, *The Lordship of Ireland in the Middle Ages* (Dublin 1972), the annates of a new approach to the history of the period which is particularly valuable for its thematic treatment even if a minor drawback is the absence of bibliography and index alike. The first want, however, is more than met by the recent publication of P. W. A. Asplin, *Medieval Ireland c. 1170-1495: A Bibliography of Secondary Works* (Dublin 1971). Economically priced and readily available, Asplin's work can be consulted with advantage by the general reader as well as the specialist, while promised from the Irish Manuscripts Commission is a no less authoritative handbook by J. F. Lydon which will do the same for the wide range of primary sources available with remarkably few exceptions in the national repositories in Dublin and London.

CHAPTER ONE

Disappointingly little has been written on the political history of this period, and a detailed appreciation of the career of Murtagh O Brien remains a *desideratum*. Much can be gleaned, however, from S. Mac Airt's edition of the *Annals of Inisfallen* (Dublin 1951), the only one of the major Irish chronicles for which there is a printed text and translation that meet the requirements of modern historical scholarship, though G. Mac Niocaill is putting the finishing touches to his completion of a comparable edition of the *Annals of Ulster* so tragically interrupted by Mac Airt's premature death. For ecclesiastical affairs there is not the same deficiency. A. Gwynn, *The Twelfth-Century Reform* (Dublin 1968) is at once attractively written and authoritative, and the same is true of the closing pages of K. W. Hughes, *The Church in Early Irish Society* (London 1966). For the rest one is very much thrown back on the original sources and on a wide range of modern literature of very uneven value, and the best introduction to the period as a whole is undoubtedly D. O Corráin, *Ireland Before the Normans* (Dublin 1972) which is specially valuable for its understanding of the problems of Leinster and of Desmond.

CHAPTER TWO

There is an extremely convenient introduction to this period in J. Ryan, *Toirdelbach O Conchubair* (Dublin 1966), and mention may also be made of B. Ó Cuív's very perceptive chapter 7 in T. W. Moody & F. X. Martin ed. *The Course of Irish History* (Cork 1967) and of the introduction contributed by K. W. Hughes to A. J. Otway-Ruthven's *History* already cited. Generally, though, one is still dependent on the Irish chronicles with the work of S. Mac Airta lighthouse in otherwise uncharted seas. Church history, however, is much better served. To the works of Gwynn and Hughes can be added the opening chapter of J. A. Watt, *The Church and the Two Nations in Medieval Ireland* (Cambridge 1970), and an excellent approach to the whole question of the coming of the Cistercians to Ireland is Dom Columcille (Ó Conbhuí) *The Story of Mellifont* (Dublin 1958). For the bull *Laudabiliter* there is an excellent point of departure in M. Sheehy's paper in *Journal of the Galway Archaeological and Historical Society* XXIX (1960-61) 45-70.

CHAPTER THREE

A stimulating if popular introduction to this period is R. Roche, *The Norman Invasion of Ireland* (Tralee 1970), and very useful is F. X. Martin's chapter 8 in *The Course of Irish History* already cited. The best setting of the Anglo-Norman invasion in its international context is undoubtedly that of W. L. Warren in *Historical Studies* VII (London 1969) 1-19. With the coming of the Anglo-Normans there is, of course, a complete change in the nature of the historical record. A new edition with English translation of the *Expugnatio* by Giraldus Cambrensis has been prepared by A. B. Scott for Brill of Leiden, and still useful even if the interpretation is controversial is G. H. Orpen, *The Song of Dermot and the Earl* (Oxford 1892). Most of the administrative documents of the new colony, too, begin to be conveniently summarised in H. S. Sweetman, *Calendar of Documents Relating to*

Ireland (London 1875-86). Other recent work on this period tends to be very specialised but mention should be made of A. J. Otway-Ruthven's general estimate of the character of the Anglo-Norman settlement in *Historical Studies* V (London 1965) 75-84.

CHAPTER FOUR

Surprisingly little work has been done on this period, but extremely useful is a work of English history, W. L. Warren's *King John* (London 1961: since reprinted as a Penguin paperback). Extraordinarily illuminating, too, is the edition of the Armagh transcript of the 1211 Pipe Roll (Irish) by O. Davies and D. B. Quinn which constituted a supplementary fascicle to volume IV (1941) of the third series of the *Ulster Archaeological Journal*. Other work has tended to be regional or biographical in scope, but mention should be made of a special study of Connacht by R. Dudley Edwards in *Irish Historical Studies* I (1938-39) 135-153 and of Papal relations by P. J. Dunning in *Journal of Ecclesiastical History*, viii (1957) 17-32.

CHAPTER FIVE

Again there is a relative paucity of material for the general reader intermediate between the excellent general accounts of Orpen, Curtis and Otway-Ruthven and more specialist discussion of individual facets of the administration in particular. The *Annals of Connacht* ed. A. M. Freeman (Dublin 1944) do go some way, however, to remedy some of the deficiency of the record, and this is perhaps the place to draw attention to some standard works on the Anglo-Norman sources. H. F. Berry, *Statutes and Ordinances and Acts of the Parliament of Ireland, King John to Henry V* (Dublin 1907) now begins usefully to supplement Sweetman, and the student will not regret dipping into the various printed *Calendars* of English as well as Irish state-papers – and particularly the Close, Patent and Pipe Rolls – which are often surprisingly rich in material relating to Ireland. H. G. Richardson & G. O. Sayles, *The Administration of Ireland 1172–1377* (Dublin 1963) largely supersedes the much more slender. material in F. M. Powicke & E. B. Fryde, *A Handbook of British Chronology* (London 1961), but the latter remains indispensable for its listing of Irish bishops. For this and the next chapter, too, J. A. Watt, *The Church and the Two Nations* already cited comes fully into its own, and there are admirable sketches of the Irish Church in the thirteenth and early fourteenth centuries in G. Hand, *The Church in the English Lordship* (Dublin 1968) and C. Mooney, *The Church in Gaelic Ireland* (Dublin 1970). K. Nicholls, *Gaelic and Gaelicised Ireland in the Middle Ages* (Dublin 1972) and J. F. Lydon, *The Lordship of Ireland* already cited give a stimulating promise of things to come, and to the various papers by Orpen, Curtis, Otway-Ruthven, Hand and Lydon listed in Asplin's *Bibliography* already cited should be added studies of the barony mearings in Cos Tipperary and Kilkenny respectively which C. A. Empey has contributed to the *North Munster Antiquarian Journal* xiii (1970) 22–29 and the *Journal of the Royal Society of Antiquaries of Ireland* ci (1971) 128–134.

CHAPTER SIX

To the works cited for the previous chapter should be added G. J. Hand, *English Law in Ireland 1290–1324* (Cambridge 1967) which is an extremely readable account embracing far more than might be thought to be indicated by the title. The Bruce invasion, too, has touched off a considerable body of literature of interest to the general reader, and mention here may be made of J. F. Lydon's masterly review of the interlude in *Historical*

Studies IV (London 1963) 111-125 which is appropriately rounded off by D. Mac Iomhair's study of the battle of Faughart in *Irish Sword* viii (1967-8) 192-209. J. F. Lydon's further paper on Edward II and the crisis in the Irish revenues in 1311 which appeared in *Irish Historical Studies* xiv (1964-5) 39-57 in fact is an excellent introduction to the period as a whole. As usual there is a shortage of biographical material, but B. Fitzgerald, *The Geraldines* (London 1951), is by no means to be despised.

GENERAL

WHAT has been essayed in the foregoing is a highly selective indication of some of the more important work in English with a special emphasis on material published over the last few years. A particularly judicious review of the work of the last generation is that by A. J. Otway-Ruthven which appears in T. W. Moody ed. *Irish Historiography 1936-70* (Dublin 1971) 16-22. Even the general reader, however, may find his interest whetted by a few specialist monographs which do not fit easily into the framework adopted. H. G. Leask, *Irish Castles and Castellated Houses* (Dundalk 1964) is a masterly introduction to the subject, and his *Irish Churches and Monastic Buildings* 3 vols (Dundalk 1955-60) is only less satisfying. Both, too, may now be supplemented by R. A. Stalley, *Architecture and Sculpture in Ireland 1150-1350* (Dublin 1971). F. Henry, *Irish Art in the Romanesque Period 1020-1170* (London 1970) is as authoritative as lavishly illustrated, and mention must be made of L. de Paor's definitive study of Cormac's Chapel in E. Rynne ed. *North Munster Studies* (Limerick 1967) 133-145. M. D. O'Sullivan, *Italian Merchant Bankers in the Thirteenth Century* (Dublin 1962) is a reminder of what remains to be done in the economic sector, and for the numismatics of the period there is now M. Dolley, *Medieval Anglo-Irish Coins*

(London 1972), though for the twelfth century 'Irish' coinages it will be necessary to wait for the promised interim report on the coins from the current excavations at High Street and Winetavern Street, Dublin.

ERRATA

p.13, l.16   This should read:—
Mac Loughlin for a year, but the death of Donal's O Brien

p.87, ll.13–15   These should read:—
Thirty years previously her father had done homage on behalf of his father to the King of Norway, and all in all it was quite a match for a young knight towards whose Ulidian conquests his liege lord was turning a blind eye. More importantly . . .

p.185, l.16   This should read:—
to intervene. On or about 10 May 1318 the Anglo-Irish

Cover illustration : The pewter pilgrims badge with the heads of SS Peter and Paul from the current High Street excavations (courtesy National Museum of Ireland)

Glossary

(Note: definitions are applicable only in the context of the present text)

ashlar: Masonry with square dressed stone laid in regular courses.

bailey: A ramparted and palisaded enclosure adjacent to a motte or tower.

barony: An Anglo-Irish administrative division of a liberty or shire.

benefice: Ecclesiastical office such as a parish or other living which confers profit on the holder.

black monk: A monk adhering to one or other of the Benedictine traditions anterior to the Cistercian reform.

burgess: The inhabitant of an incorporated town ('borough') enjoying rights and privileges including a voice in the election of its officials.

cantred: A division of territory usually corresponding to but by no means conterminous with a later barony.

caput: The chief castle of an honour.

castle: A defensive work, originally of earth and timber and later of stone, housing a garrison and capable of indefinite resistance to an army without a siege-train.

charter: Document setting out formally the terms on which a fee or fief is held.

cleric: A person in holy orders, not necessarily a bishop, priest or monk.

coarb: The successor of the founder of a see or monastery with full rights over its endowments although not necessarily a bishop or priest.

collegiate church: A church where, as in a cathedral, the revenues are shared between a number of canons but which is not the cathedral of a bishop.

concubinage: The living together of a man and woman outside formal marriage.

crannog: A small lake-island, often artificial, adapted as a fortified residence.

dower-land: Property settled on a wife by her husband at their marriage and in which she retained rights after his death.

erenagh: A hereditary tenant of land originally given to the Church, and enjoying quasi-clerical status although not in major orders.

fee, fief: A grant of property conditional on the fulfilment of certain obligations of a primarily military nature.

fifths, historic: The five major divisions of Gaelic Ireland before the Anglo-Norman invasion, Connacht, Munster and Ulster more or less corresponding to the modern provinces of the same name, and Leinster and Meath broadly representing the southern and northern halves respectively of the modern Leinster.

filiation: The daughter-houses founded from and subordinate to a particular Cistercian monastery.

gallowglass: A mailed and axe-bearing mercenary of Scotto-Norse descent and trained to fight in a formation capable of withstanding a cavalry-charge.

hierarchy: The European norm of national Church-government with a primate, metropolitans, bishops etc.

homage: The formal acknowledgement of another as king or liege or mesne lord.

honour: Grouping of fiefs or fees in the hands of a single lord under the king.

justiciar: The Anglo-Norman chief governor of Ireland under the Lord of Ireland as such.

king's hand: The exercise by the king of his right to adminster and enjoy the profits from fiefs during the minority of an heir.

knight: A heavy cavalryman usually providing his own horses, weapons and keep for a fixed period each year in return for a grant of land on favourable terms.

knight-service: The discharge of the obligation on a fief to provide one or more knights for the feudal host.

liberty: An honour or fief where the administration of Justice was left with only a few exceptions to the tenant-in-chief.

liege: Feudal superior.

mark: A money of account or bar of silver of the value of 160 pennies.

mearing: Boundary or landmark.

mesne: Feudal superior intermediate between the vassal and a great lord or the king.

metropolitan: An archbishop with jurisdiction over a number of bishops.

monogamy: The Christian ideal of marriage where a man or woman is married to a single partner for his or her life.

motte: The early form of castle where a massive mound of earth is topped by a palisade and lofty wooden tower.

pallium: A special form of stole reserved for metropolitans and dispatched to them by the Pope as a mark of his approbation of their exercise of provincial jurisdiction.

paruchia: An Irish grouping of originally more or less independent monasteries in subordination to a major house which could offer protection from lay spoliation.

patrimony: The lands traditionally endowing a particular religious house.

primate: Archbishop exercising a measure of jurisdiction over the other metropolitans of a national Church.

sanctuary: An immunity from arrest conferred by physical presence in a given place most usually a church or shrine.

scutage: A money payment on occasion made by a vassal in place of knight-service.

seneschal: Steward appointed by a major lord to look after his interests in a particular fief or castle.

sheriff: A royal official with a general supervision of royal rights within a given shire.

shire: An administrative division, corresponding more or less to a modern county, where the administration of justice was substantially reserved to royal courts.

simony: Thr trafficking for private profit in ecclesiastical offices.

temporalities: The secular profits and other privileges accruing to a see or monastery from its possession of church-lands.

tenant-in-chief: A vassal holding an honour or other major fief directly of the king without the inter-position of a mesne lord.

tithe: A tax on property of a tenth of its annual render payable to the parish-church.

vassal: The holder of a fee or fief.

visitation: The formal inspection of a see or of its component benefices by a metropolitan or bishop or his deputy, or of a religious house by a superior from outside.

writ: A written instruction from the king.

Index

209